ADVERTISERS ANONYMOUS

ADVERTISERS ANONYMOUS

12 Steps
TO CREATIVE SALVATION

RON HUEY

Published by Ripples Media
Atlanta, Georgia
www.ripples.media

Copyright © 2026 by Ron Huey

All rights reserved. No part of this book may be reproduced or used in any manner without written permission of the copyright owner except for the use of quotations in a book review.

For more information: contact@ripples.media

First printing 2026

Book and cover design by Burtch Hunter

ISBN (Paperback) 979-1-971718-06-4
ISBN (Hardcover) 979-1-971718-07-1
ISBN (eBook) 979-1-971718-05-7

*To my parents, my wife Judy,
daughter Alex and son Nic—
with love and gratitude.*

FOREWORD

by Ernie Schenck

I suspect Ron asked me to write this foreword because we've known each other for years, worked in the same circles, but mostly because our creative sensibilities lie pretty much on the same frequency. When he sent the manuscript, he said, "Just read it and say whatever you think, but don't make it sound like an award-show speech."

Yeah. That's Ron.

I read the book in one sitting. I put it down, thought about it for a day, and read it again. What struck me most is how completely it sounds like the guy I've known for a long time. No grand pronouncements. No pretending he has all the answers. No attempt to position himself as the grizzled elder on the mountaintop. Just a long, clear-eyed conversation from someone who's spent his entire career doing great work.

I'll tell you this.

The book feels like you're sitting across a table from Ron after hours, when the office is quiet and everyone's guard is down. He talks about the craft with respect, with humor when it's warranted, and with zero patience for anything that gets in the way of a clean, human idea. He writes about the daily reality of making things. The excitement when something clicks so damn loud, you think it's going to blow up in your face. The frustration when it doesn't.

What comes through on every page is a deep, steady belief that advertising, at its best, is still a craft that deserves to be taken seriously. Deserves? Hell, no. Demands. Not because it can save the world, but because when it's done right, it can surprise people. Move them to tears. Make them laugh. Make them question. He never romanticizes the struggle, but he refuses to dismiss it either.

If you've ever cared about doing work that feels honest, if you've ever fought for an idea you believed in, if you've ever walked out of a meeting wondering whether any of it still matters, this book will feel like a long conversation with someone who understands exactly where you are and refuses to let you settle for less than you're capable of.

They're not easy to come by, those conversations. Especially not with someone the likes of Ron Huey. The voice in these pages is the same voice I've come to know over these many years. It's kind when it needs to be, tough when it has to be, and always, always focused on the work.

Ron, thank you for writing this. Thank you for trusting me to introduce it. And thank you for never letting cynicism have the last word.

Do yourself a favor, young padawan. Settle in. Get comfortable. Grab a cold one. Grab a highlighter. Because as Bill Bernbach is my witness, you're going to learn things.

Ernie Schenck
Creative Director, columnist for *Communication Arts* and author of the *Strange Alchemy* newsletter and *The Houdini Solution*

PREFACE

This job of creativity is a rocky, but rewarding road.
It takes discipline, rigor, resolve and plenty more.

The 12 Steps of *Advertisers Anonymous*
are character traits that I've found helpful
through both success and failure.

The passages are meant to be short,
simple daily reminders. Hopefully, things you can
carry with you every step of your career.

*"You can't wait for inspiration,
you have to go after it with a club."*

– Jack London

12 Steps

PERSEVERANCE / 1

DILIGENCE / 21

AMBITION / 55

TRUST / 79

HUMILITY / 103

PERSPECTIVE / 125

HONESTY / 153

INITIATIVE / 183

DISCIPLINE / 207

INGENUITY / 233

GRATITUDE / 251

ACCEPTANCE / 267

ADVERTISERS ANONYMOUS

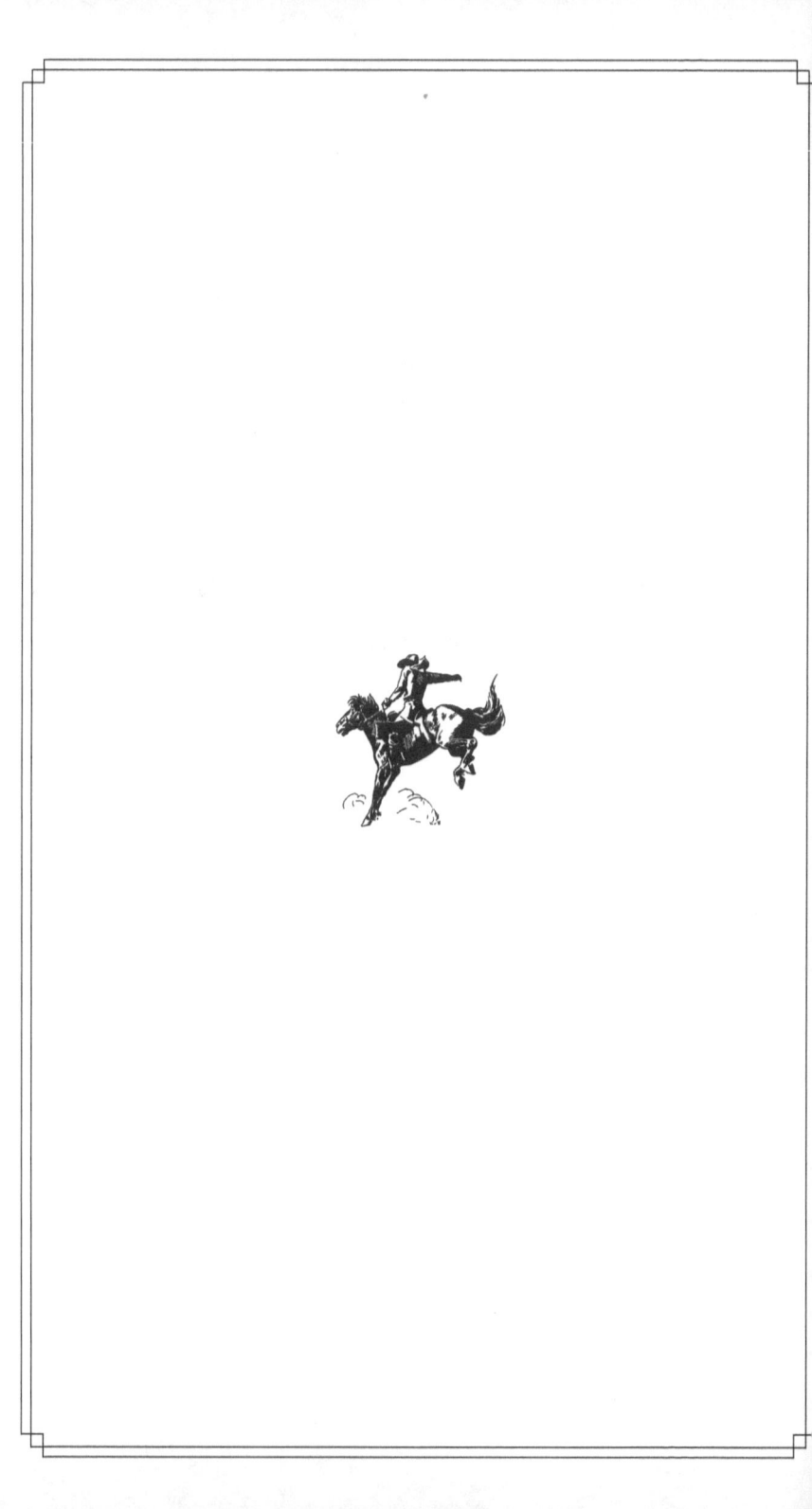

Step 1

PERSEVERANCE

Advertising is a bucking bronco

hellbent on tossing you head over heels.

Are you willing to climb back on?

THICK SKIN

The B-52's, an enigmatic Athens, Georgia rock band, hit the late 1970s music scene like an atomic bomb.

Their sound was different, quirky, unruly and unapologetic.

Not everyone was a fan.

The B-52's kicked open the doors for many Athens' musical artists to follow, including Pylon, Widespread Panic, Drive-By Truckers and REM.

They all had something to say. Like it or not.

One of my favorite Athens' bands, The Vigilantes of Love, gained a bit of notoriety with their album, *Welcome to Struggleville.*

In their song, "*Skin*," they warned, "*You better bring your thickest skin.*"

The line was an observation of Vincent Van Gogh and the reality that every artist must face: criticism.

Whether you're a painter, poet, musician, or perhaps, an advertising creative, your work will be judged, scrutinized and picked apart by those who can't do what you can.

Be prepared to hear that your babies are ugly.

[PERSEVERANCE]

That your ideas are ill-conceived.

That your magic is running short.

It's okay. In fact, it's what you're signing up for. Creativity will always be subjective. There isn't a right or wrong answer, only judgment.

This isn't an occupation for whiners.

Having your work constantly stretched about like taffy can be disheartening and exhausting, but the best creatives are incredibly resilient.

They have to be.

Welcome to Struggleville, my friend.

THE WHITE BULL

Ernest Hemingway famously once called the blank page a "white bull," a menacing creature that creatives had to face down and subjugate somehow, in the pursuit of producing new works.

It's the idea that no matter how well you wrote the day before, or what kind of art you created weeks ago, no matter how lauded your past efforts have been, there is always a fresh sheet of paper or stretch of canvas that will stare you down the next time, either enticing you or taunting you to do it all over again.

The responsibility of being a creative can be intimidating. It can and will make your gut churn. It's not easy. For those of us who do it for a living, we know that it's not all fun and games. Our reputation is on the line with each assignment.

The good news is that, over time, you'll learn to trust your talent and instincts.

Start every assignment with just getting words and ideas down on paper. Get the ball rolling, don't filter. Ideas lead to more ideas.

When writing copy, get your points down clearly, get the building blocks in place, then figure out how to make it more engaging and more creative.

[PERSEVERANCE]

As long as you work in this business, every new assignment will feel imposing. Your experience will quiet the fear. Your brain will learn to untangle the ropes.

The more you do it, the less you will wonder about your ability to solve it.

When facing the white bull, creativity is your red cape.

KNOCK THREE TIMES. FOUR, IF NEEDED.

I wanted a job as a copywriter. Badly. Not just anywhere, but in a great agency.

Only a few years out of college, I had tunneled my way out of a junior account service position and into the free world of creative. My fledgling portfolio was a poor work-in-progress. Duct tape and hope.

I sent it off to Mike Hughes, legendary Creative Director of The Martin Agency in Richmond. An advertising Hall-of-Famer and giant of the business.

Not hiring, Mike's reply and advice was clear and so true: "Stay in touch. Ours is a business known for change."

Whether it's of your own choosing or not, change is inevitable.

Agencies hire and fire all the time. It's a revolving door. One week, a big client bolts and staff is dumped like oversized baggage. The next, a big pitch is won and new hires are furiously added like eager ants to a picnic.

Our business is volatile to say the least.

Over five years passed after receiving the note from Mike. 1,825 days to be exact.

[PERSEVERANCE]

Like he asked, I stayed in touch with him and others at the agency, sharing new work samples, complimenting their new work and simply saying, "Hi."

When they won the Mercedes-Benz account, Mike and Kerry Feuerman hired me to help steer the creative work, and tossed me the keys.

Patience and persistence had paid off.

Make contacts, stay in touch and keep knocking. You never know when a sheet metal door might spring open.

CALLOUSED FINGERS

The art of sharp, thought-provoking writing will never go out of style, regardless of platform or pixel count. Great writing is eternal.

Crafting memorable headlines, copy, and scripts isn't a 100-yard dash. It requires pounding and pounding on your keyboard. Bend your thoughts this way and that. Rearrange them. Rip them apart and reassemble them. Keep digging. Keep chiseling.

Falling in love with your first thoughts is easy, especially when they're well-received by others. This is a danger. It may feel like the finish line, but it's just the starting gun. Great writing and ideas are born from great rigor.

Bob Cianfrone, a young, hungry writer and casualty of a crosstown agency layoff, was paying his bills swinging a hammer on construction sites when his portfolio caught our eye at our agency, Huey/Paprocki. Upon meeting him, his humble, roll-up-your-sleeves attitude sealed the deal.

Construction and advertising have a lot in common. Things are built one board, one brick, one nail at a time.

We brought Bob in and handed him a challenge: writing headlines for our client, Nancy Lopez Golf. Barely a few days passed before Bob dropped a stack of paper on our desk.

[PERSEVERANCE]

Over 20 pages of headlines, single spaced.

That's over 300 headlines if my math is correct. There were many good ones and a small handful of amazing ones.

Over the next two years, Bob cranked out award-winning work that raised eyebrows and turned heads across the industry. Crispin Porter + Bogusky, one of the hottest shops in the country, soon came calling and lured Bob away.

We hated to see him go, but we were proud, too. His work helped put our growing agency on the national radar. And gave Bob a future site to swing a bigger hammer.

THREE-HOLED BOWLING BALLS

Knowing when "good enough" is actually good enough might be the hardest part of being creative. You'll never turn over every stone. There's always another idea hiding under the next rock, whispering, "Hey, genius, you missed me."

Luke Sullivan – ad legend and author of *Hey Whipple, Squeeze This*—professed that all you need each day is one three-holed bowling ball.

Luke's point was that a one-holed or two-holed bowling ball was virtually useless. You can't grip it. You can't roll it straight. Most ideas are flawed in some way or another.

But a three-holed bowling ball? That's close to perfection.

Luke suggested that, for a full day of concepting, your goal is to walk away with one idea that has everything going for it.

Brilliant and bulletproof.

A whole day's effort for just one strike-worthy concept. Sounds easy, but it's not.

The best creatives are constantly digging, looking to discard good ideas for even better ones. They never stop thinking, questioning or exploring.

They resist the temptation to feel like they've solved it.

[PERSEVERANCE]

There are two words in this business that can drop you faster than black ice: "That's great."

You might hear this from classmates, account partners, creative directors—even clients.

"That's great" sounds like validation. Like your work is done here. But it's a trap.

"That's great" is a warm, fuzzy blanket that lulls you into creative complacency urging you to quit digging, stop pushing.

Bowling balls or ad concepts, keep drilling down and polishing. Only you will know when you've hit perfection.

CHASE HAPPINESS

Clients are a necessity, but the brands you choose to work with is up to you. This is especially true when running your own shop.

At Huey/Paprocki, working on a golf brand was for us the holy grail. As luck would have it, Mizuno's North American headquarters was just a short, 15-mile drive north of our office in Atlanta.

But getting through their door was about as difficult as getting up and down from a greenside bunker.

Every few months, we'd package up some of our best work and try to tunnel in digitally or by the good 'ol U.S. Mail. Still, our follow-up calls to Lisa Mark, the marketing contact there, seemed to fall on deaf ears.

Then, one day, our phone unexpectedly rang.

I sat in astonishment as I listened, "Hi, this is Lisa Mark at Mizuno USA. How are you?" She continued, "I've been impressed with the work you've sent over the past few months. We just haven't had a project that was a good fit for your agency. We do now. Could you meet with us in the coming week?"

This news hit squarely on the sweet spot.

[PERSEVERANCE]

For all we knew, Lisa hated the work. She never returned our calls. Yet we methodically stuck to our plan of putting our best work under her nose and the sniff test paid off.

Over seven years, working with Lisa and her team, we produced a wheelbarrow's worth of award-winning, market-share boosting work across Mizuno's golf, running and diamond divisions.

Regardless of your sport; practice, repetition, and building consistency are keys to success.

It's the same for your agency's new business game.

MAKING PRETZELS

Headlines are meant to be twisted. They rarely roll off the tongue or keyboard in their perfect form.

They are merely rough thoughts, often smart and good, but they haven't been explored, crafted or molded yet.

The raw ingredients may be there, but their true form hasn't taken shape.

AI and ChatGPT can be useful in serving up variations on your thoughts. But be prepared to trim and tighten even those suggestions.

The exercise of writing great lines is an arduous one. While AI is a great tool, don't use it as a crutch. Don't expect AI to do the work for you. Your brain needs to do some heavy lifting. Or atrophy will set it.

You'd be amazed how many different ways you can say the same thing and you must explore each and every twist and turn. Chew thoroughly. Take where you start and make that where you end. Dig into the thesaurus, scrub every word.

Start by just getting thoughts on paper, as many as you can in rapid fire succession.

There will be plenty of time to revisit, rethink and retwist.

[PERSEVERANCE]

For me, it takes at least three or four pages of lines before I start to pluck out some that have merit. And still, even those are likely half-baked.

Even the lines that make the 'short list' still need to be turned and turned again to reveal the best, most succinct version of each thought.

If you have a creative director worthy of their corner office, they'll push you. But the real push has to come from you.

The only way to know that you've said it perfectly is to explore every possible iteration.

Headlines are a little like snow globes. They need to be constantly shaken to see where the words might land.

The same is true for art direction and design.

Shuffling elements, exploring fonts, point sizes, background textures can, and should be, a relentless pursuit.

Give yourself the time you need to consider all your options.

Keep twisting and you'll know when you get there.

SEVEN TIMES A CHARM

There are iconic advertising campaigns that are seared into our memories over time. For me, the famous "Red Border" campaign for *Time* magazine, created by Art Director Bob Barrie and Copywriter Dean Buckhorn, made me realize just how high the creative bar is set.

Brilliant in its simplicity and beauty, the campaign took the magazine's simple red cover border and strategically used it to frame an element of one of their stunning images.

The photos were jaw-dropping. The words, pointed and piercing.

If you don't know about this campaign, you should.

One ad featured a photo of Jacqueline Kennedy Onassis swinging her young daughter over the ocean waves. The headline read: "In an era of tabloid journalism, we believe the truth to be sensational enough."

Another, showing an airport security guard scanning a five-year-old kid with a metal detector with the line: "At what point do national security and common sense collide?"

The sheer simplicity and ingenious mechanics of the idea gave it legs like a centipede, spawning over 200 executions.

Not surprisingly, the campaign won every award imaginable.

[PERSEVERANCE]

Including being named Print Campaign of the Decade by *The One Show*.

What was surprising?

The creative team was sent back to the drawing board seven times. That's not a typo. Multiple campaigns died before this most famous one was granted life.

If there ever was a testament to the rewards of perseverance, this is it.

You will be knocked down. Brush it off. There's another great idea out there.

You never know. Your next one might be written into advertising history.

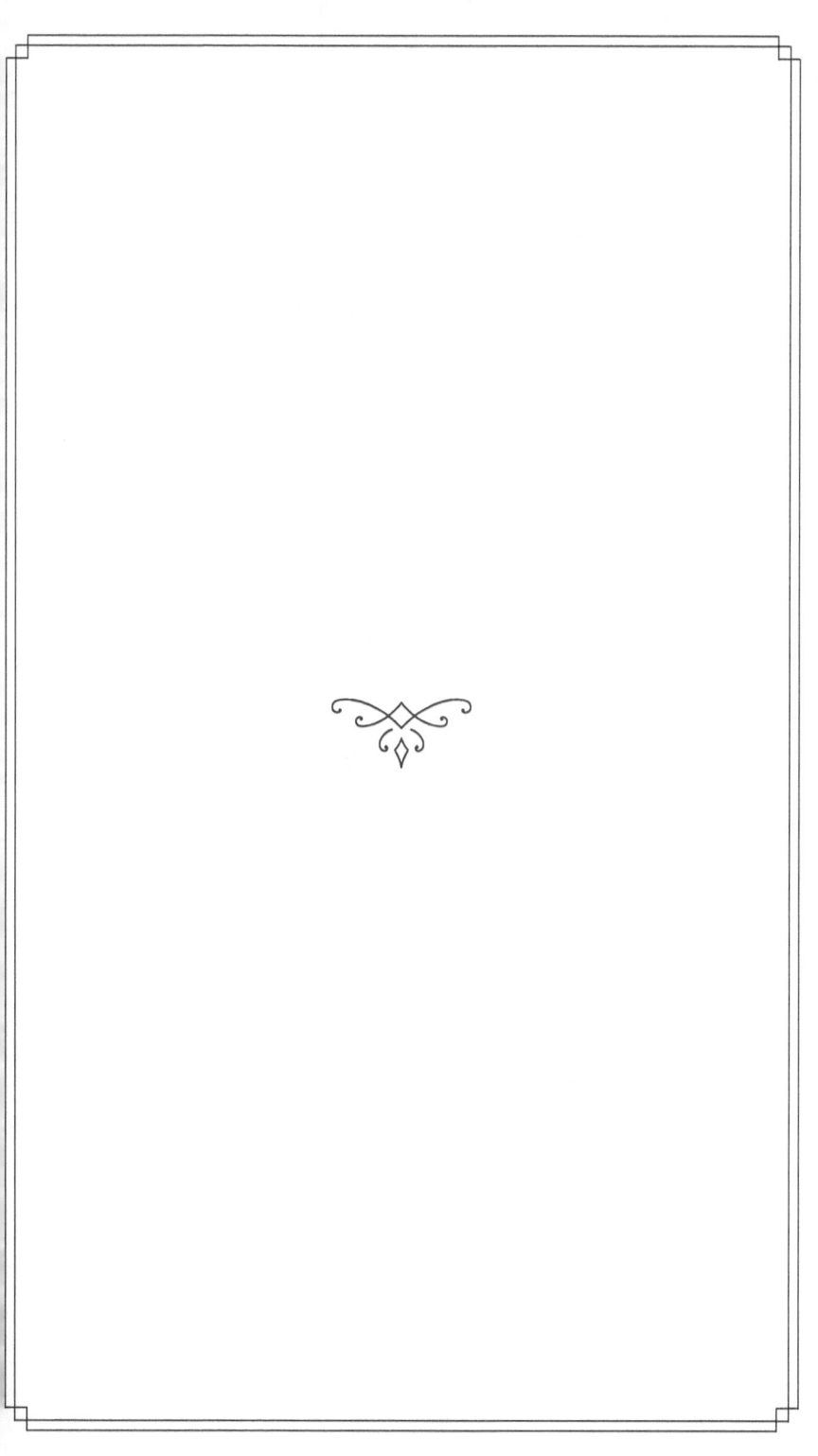

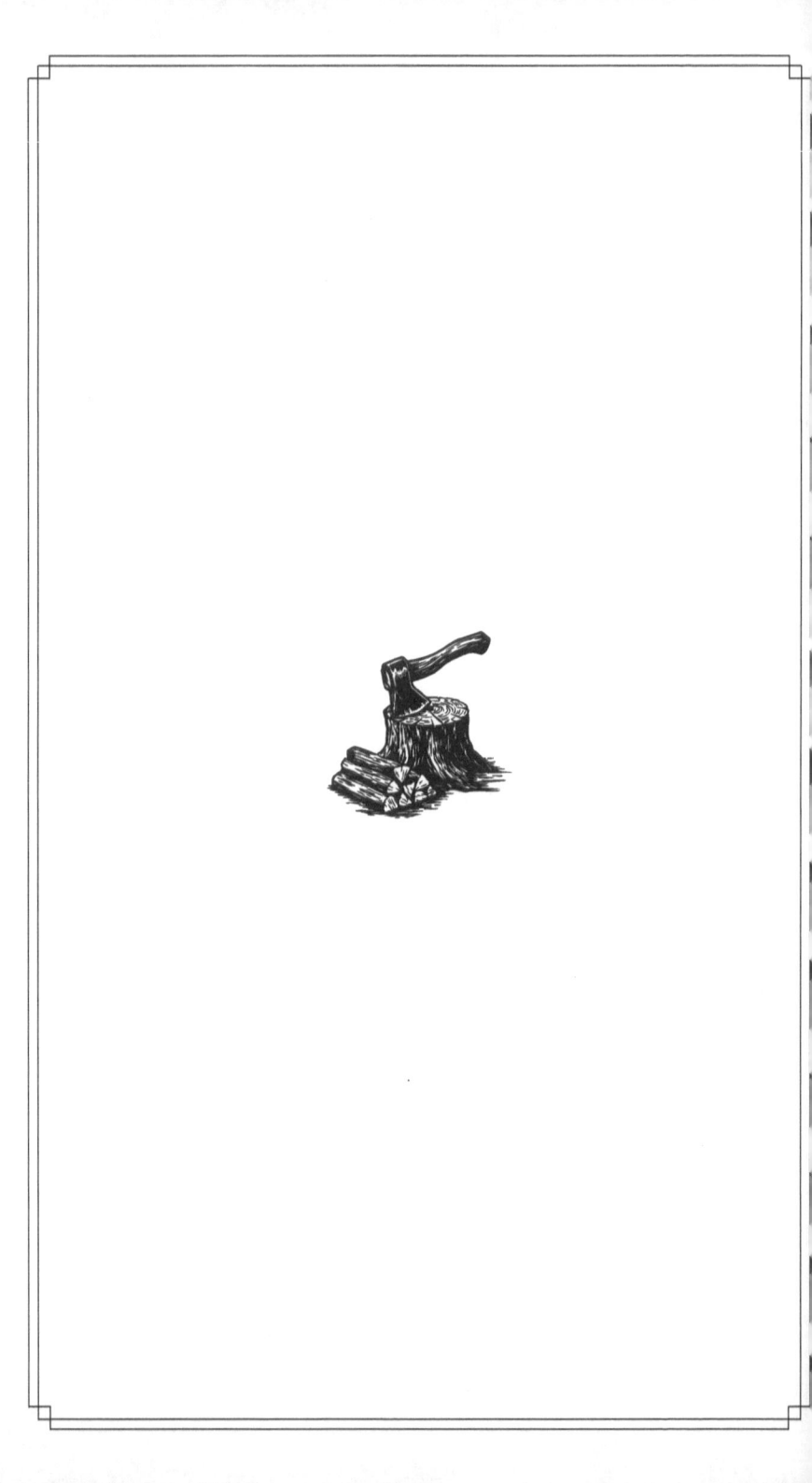

Step 2

DILIGENCE

Great work will not come easy.

It is born from sweat and hard work.

Stay focused and keep swinging.

STUDY YOUR HEROES

◆

Tony Gwynn, a fifteen-time MLB All-Star and Hall-of-Famer, was one of the greatest hitters of the last century. He won eight batting titles, a feat equaled only by the immortal Honus Wagner, who broke into the league in 1897.

Gwynn didn't invent hitting. He learned to hit by studying the art of hitting, by idolizing and dissecting the great hitters before him. He spent hours watching tapes of the great Ted Williams' swing and tried to model it.

Having heroes and mentors is important. In any business.

To learn the craft of writing, I studied those I greatly admired: Jerry Cronin, Luke Sullivan and Rod Kilpatrick. I tried to emulate their style, their wit and their insight until I developed a style I could call my own.

As a creative stalwart at Portland's Wieden+Kennedy, Jerry Cronin churned out award-winning work for ESPN, Nike, and others. For Nike Running, Jerry's elegant takes embodied Nike's "Just Do It" brand mantra.

One image showed a long stretch of open road with body copy which read: "There are clubs you can't belong to. Neighborhoods you can't live in. Schools you can't get into. But the roads are always open. Just do it."

[DILIGENCE]

Another haunting image captured a lone runner crossing a darkened bridge with a full moon rising in the background. The body copy read: "Mothers, there's a madman running in the streets. And he's humming a tune. And he's snarling at dogs. And he still has four more miles to go. Just do it."

These ads didn't speak to product attributes like wider widths or foam cushioning. They spoke to the soul of a runner.

Rod Kilpatrick's iconic work was required reading for me as I climbed up the ranks. Headlines like "Money talks. We translate." for the *Wall Street Journal* or poetic lines for Murray's like: "In these trendy times, restaurants rise and fall as fast as a kiwi souffle on a muggy afternoon."

There was thought and an art poured into each and every word.

Remember, you're not starting from scratch in this business, there are plenty of others who've stood in the batter's box. We can all learn from those who routinely knocked it out of the park.

YOU'RE A BUSINESS PARTNER

Creatives like to live in our own little bubble of quick-witted comebacks, punk rock t-shirts and retro sneakers.

But smart clients expect more from us than funny lines and hip Spotify playlists.

They want us to get their business—to actually care about what keeps them up at night. To roll up our sleeves and get down in the muck.

Truth is, the more we know about all aspects of our client's business, the more powerful our creative arsenal becomes.

I've seen too many creatives tune out in client meetings when the channel flips from the creative work to more stimulating topics like media flow charts, market share bar graphs and sales force collateral needs.

I get it, death by PowerPoint is about as appealing as a sharp stick in the eye. But clients notice.

To be creative, you have to be strategic. The best creatives aren't just artists, they're brand architects. Some of the most strategic thinkers in the room.

When your ideas are rooted in strategy, they're virtually bulletproof.

[DILIGENCE]

Our creative minds can solve much more than what fits on a page or a screen. We're here to solve tough business challenges, not just relay product benefits.

Our outside observations about non-creative things are incredibly valuable.

Seeing your client's business from every angle makes you more than a creative partner, it makes you their secret weapon.

THIN THE HERD

Great ideas come from lots and lots of good ideas. When diving into an assignment, get as many rough ideas on your wall as early as possible.

Quality will come from quantity.

Keep your presentation date clearly in your crosshairs, leave yourself enough time to identify your strongest ideas and tighten them up.

It's great to share a range of thinking in client meetings. It not only flexes your creative muscles, but shows you're not a one-trick pony.

But this is no place for Chinese menus. Too many choices and too many options creates too much confusion.

For me, sharing three to five campaign directions seemed to be the right amount. Each with a clear, unique angle and appeal. Show how each concept can work across a variety of mediums.

But don't mandate how many directions to show, let the work dictate that. If you only have three strong directions, show those. If you have five you'd love to produce, show all five.

Whatever the number, walk into the presentation knowing you'd be happy if they bought any of the campaigns.

[DILIGENCE]

Many agencies may push to have a 'safe' option in the mix. It's okay to have a safe option if that option is brilliant.

Brilliant and buyable isn't a bad place to be.

McDonald's produces a lot of warm and fuzzy stuff. And they often do it amazingly well.

Clients can only buy what you're selling. Make sure everything you put on the menu is great for them and great for you.

CROOKED THINGS

When concepting, here's a simple rule to live by: Crooked visuals need straight headlines. And crooked headlines need straight visuals.

Your visual can be incredibly creative or your headline can be. But don't try to make them both too clever. It often complicates and slows down communication.

In the early days of high-speed internet, we were hired by a commercial real estate company putting fiber lines in all their new office buildings. They needed a campaign touting their ultra-high-speed advantage.

Working with a table top sculptor, we built a small skeleton shaped like a computer mouse, tiny rib cages and all. We photographed it in all its bare bones glory on a mouse pad. It was no doubt an arresting visual.

The headline read: *Get a faster internet connection.* Nothing cute or fancy, just right to the point. The visual did all the creative heavy lifting.

For our client, The Atlanta History Center, we needed an ad promoting Teacher Appreciation Week. We got access to a local grocery store and took a photo of the produce rack with the apples section completely empty. An intriguing visual for sure.

[DILIGENCE]

The straight line beneath it read: *Teacher Appreciation Week // May 6–13.*

When the Atlanta Hawks looked to promote their new lineup, we produced an outdoor board with point guard, Jeff Teague, driving to the hoop. Nothing particularly catchy about the photo. The billboard was placed on one of Atlanta's busiest highways. The headline read: *Drives like a maniac..*

Crooked lines or crooked visuals—both approaches work. Just don't marry the two.

WE'RE ALL BUSY

Between life and work, there is rarely time to pump the brakes. It's easy to feel overwhelmed, sucked into the undertow and drowning in a sea of endless meetings and deadlines.

Such is the life of a creative.

Worse yet, creative types can be known for procrastination.

But the ability to manage our time and workload is our only escape route to sanity. The most successful creatives can clock out of the chaos and find ways to organize.

They don't use "being busy" as a crutch because they know that everyone else is just as busy. No pity party here.

So what's the secret?

Clear off the non-creative tasks first. When I make to-do lists and check them off, I feel pretty darn productive. More importantly, getting the busy work out of the way allows me to focus on the creative work that really needs time and attention.

Being busy doesn't give us the excuse to completely disappear. Stay in touch and stay plugged in.

Make time to return emails and phone calls, don't leave

[DILIGENCE]

people hanging. Be respectful by being on time and responsible.

We're in the people business. You want your colleagues to respect you. Because when they respect you, they'll respect your thinking.

Let's shatter the stereotype of the whiny and unorganized creative.

Run your life and your work with purpose and efficiency.

It's great preparation for running an agency—if that's where this crazy dream leads you.

SIDESWIPED

There is a code of ethics among the best creatives. They're students of the game and well aware of the creative work out in the world.

The concept of stealing someone else's idea doesn't compute for most because they know they'll be called out. Labeled a fraud.

But apparently, this creative code of ethics isn't universally embraced.

I'd recently returned from presenting TV concepts to our Mercedes-Benz client. It was a good meeting and they bought a nice concept, it just wasn't my favorite of the bunch.

The idea I loved was incredibly simple and powerful, but the client chose a different route. It happens.

I was working in Richmond and one of my former partners was freelancing at a well-known West Coast agency with a rival car account.

We were in touch and I casually mentioned my meeting with my Mercedes client, lamenting the fact that they didn't pick the concept I loved.

It's common for creatives to mourn the dead. The ones that got away.

[DILIGENCE]

Six months later, my phone rang. On the other end, my old partner quietly asked, "Are you sitting down? I just saw your Mercedes concept on Monday Night Football for another car company."

Huh? What?

Then he fessed up. While freelancing, he had mentioned my passed-over concept to another creative working there. Apparently, someone figured the idea was up for grabs and decided to adopt it as their own and presented it to their automotive client.

I can't blame the client for approving and producing it. As I mentioned, it was a simple, powerful idea.

In the car business, ideas can accidentally overlap. This didn't feel like that. The timing here was too coincidental. This felt more like a creative car-jacking in plain sight.

I learned that day: keep your ideas close to the vest. On the highway of creative integrity, it's easy to get sideswiped.

SLEEP ON IT

Few things done fast are done well. Ideas need time to breathe, to ferment, to be poked, prodded and put on trial.

It's why the creative process demands time and rigor.

And sleep.

Your brain isn't a 24-hour diner. Our mind and body need a break to recharge. A good night's sleep gives us a new perspective. Ideas that seemed like late night brilliance often appear as pumpkins in the early morning light.

The mantra, "Nothing good happens after midnight." certainly applies to creative concepting.

Somewhere along the line, our industry took a wrong turn down the dark alley of ridiculous pitch deadlines, all-nighters and caffeine-fueled panic.

All of which amounts to creative burnout, not brilliance.

When your brain is forced to churn like a hamster on a wheel, it tires, it loses perspective, it starts to spit out mush. It also loses out on the opportunity to wake up refreshed, sharp, and curious.

Some of our best thinking comes when just waking in that weird limbo state between consciousness and dreamland.

[DILIGENCE]

Many mornings, I've rolled over only to be hit right between my sand-soaked eyes with an idea that I'd been trying to solve for weeks.

There will be times when burning the midnight oil is unavoidable, but try to make it the rare exception.

Give your mind the rest it needs and it will pay you back many times over.

ORDER UP!

Clients often want things fast. But much like a McDonald's cheeseburger, fast isn't always appetizing, fulfilling, or even good for you.

Every assignment is different. Some are quick hits that can be knocked out whack-a-mole style. But great thinking requires time to reflect and rethink.

Creativity hates being rushed.

When a client asks, "Can I see something back by the end of day?" my response is, "Sure, but I can't promise it's going to be any good."

Good work takes time. That's just a fact.

Unlike a tasty pint of lager, you can't simply pull the tap and let creativity pour freely.

Which is why finding smart clients and account partners who understand and value the creative process is critical.

Some agencies have figured this out better than others.

Agencies and companies led by creative thinkers understand what great work takes: time, direction and a culture that puts creativity above convenience.

[DILIGENCE]

When everyone in the company, not just the creative department, believes inspired, memorable work is what drives success, then you've got something special.

But that belief always has to come from the top down.

The direction and leadership has to come from the brilliant thinkers, not the bean counters.

On the client side, marketing has to be valued within the company and seen as a way to differentiate the brand, provide support for the sales team and grow the business.

This isn't always the case.

So choose your clients carefully, protect your timelines and guard your process.

We're not magicians, much less short-order cooks.

GETTING STIFFED

Let's be clear, this is a transactional business. We're hired for our insights, intelligence and creativity. We interpret research. We apply science. We make art. We build brands.

And we deserve to be paid fairly for it.

It seems easy enough. You do the work, you get the check. No different than trading a bushel of corn for a coonskin hat, but it doesn't always go that way.

New clients can be dangerously seductive. Maybe it's a dream brand you've wanted to work on forever. Maybe the marketing team seems like your kind of people: friendly, flattering, "We just *love* your work."

But before you're swept off your creative feet, remember a handshake and good vibes don't pay the bills.

Whether you're a freelancer or a 200-person agency, get the paperwork in order before you lift a creative finger. Early on, I used a simple two-page "Letter of Agreement" that clearly outlined the deliverables, revision limits, timing and payment terms. Clear and simple.

Getting the right agreement in place is nothing to apologize for. You have a business to run. Good clients respect the process while bad clients exploit chaos.

[DILIGENCE]

And chaos always starts small. A client asked for a simple scoop of vanilla, but now wants nuts, gummy bears and a cherry on top. That's reality.

Stay on top of your estimates, amend and rescope as needed. Track your time.

If payment is lagging, pump the brakes, stop the presses.

A little extra concepting time is one thing, production costs are another altogether.

Fronting hard costs to production or edit houses is a disaster waiting to strike. I've seen this mistake literally wipe agencies off the face of the advertising map.

It's one thing to lose the cost of your thinking, it's another to lose retirement savings.

Concerning money matters, trust no one.

Not until the ink's dry and the deposit's cleared.

THINK TANKS

Creativity has migrated over the decades from pen and pad to laptops and 32-inch, 6K retina display monitors.

It's a beautiful thing, for sure, but often it helps to go old school and literally paper the walls.

Creative thinking wants to be visible. Tangible. Something you can walk up to, grab a black marker, and scribble notes and thoughts.

Treat your workspace like a think tank. Immerse yourself in your own chaos. Whether it's rough comps from the computer or doodles on a napkin, pin them up.

Stare at them incessantly. Judge them. Re-judge them. Keep them under constant critique.

Try to carve out different strategic paths, all leading to the bullseye in the creative brief. Group like-minded ideas and headline thoughts together.

Turn your workspace into a bubbling cauldron of words, visuals, sketches, sticky notes and random inspiration.

This is truly the time to throw ideas against the walls and see what sticks. Put stars on ideas that are working, question marks on those that need more work. Make your wall feel alive.

[DILIGENCE]

Visual stimulation wakes the senses. Tactile things still count for something. Don't just think, physically wrestle with the ideas. Move them around. Mash them up. Rip them apart. Reassemble them.

As campaigns begin to gel, sharpen them on the computer. Print new comps, update the wall. Tear down the losers. Rinse and repeat.

Don't waste too much time *trying* to make ideas work. Strong ideas will naturally come together. They easily demonstrate how and why they're strong. Big ideas are easily extendable. That becomes quickly obvious.

It's a little bit like "King of the Mountain" where your strongest ideas fend off challengers until only the best and brightest are left standing.

DANDELIONS

Unfortunately, the creative brain doesn't come with a convenient on/off switch. It would be nice if it were that simple.

Our creative minds work in funny ways. Even when you unplug, your brain doesn't. It keeps sparking, spinning and tossing things around long after you've clocked out.

That's why being a creative is a 24-hour job. Because you never know which hour the idea might strike.

Ideas don't care about fitting neatly into your daily calendar. They're on their own schedule and capable of knocking at any time.

Even when you're trying to sleep.

Even when you just want a shower.

Even when you're running errands or mowing the lawn.

Even when your vacation is finally here, your creative brain remains on the clock.

But when ideas do come, and they will, capture them in the moment.

Don't just make a mental note assuming you'll remember

[DILIGENCE]

it later when you get back to your computer. Or tomorrow when you get back to concepting.

Get it down while it's fresh in your mind. Every part, every piece, every detail. Because it will escape you.

It may be the way a headline is structured. Or a funny line of dialogue that completes a scene.

Make a note on your phone. Scribble it down on a grocery receipt. Leave a voice memo. I often send myself a text.

Whatever it is, don't trust it to memory.

Ideas are like dandelions. They're only perfect once. And the wind's gonna blow.

CLEAN YOUR BRUSHES

I was walking along a city street in Bern, Switzerland, surrounded by the familiar hum of passing vehicles, flashing traffic lights and shuffling pedestrians, but something was different here. I couldn't quite put my finger on it, then my eyes solved the mystery.

Along the sidewalks, where crews had spent their day jackhammering concrete to smithereens and tunneling through asphalt, the worker's tools had been neatly stacked to the side. The sidewalks swept so clean and spotless you could eat a Kanelbulle off them. Their day's labor was wrapped, tidied up and ready for tomorrow.

We're only as good as our tools and our daily habits.

Anyone who's ever slung paint on a house or a canvas knows the rule: take care of your brushes, take care of your work.

The same goes for concepting, writing, editing or designing. When you walk away, leave things in a good place.

Some preach that creativity is born from chaos. Maybe for some, that works. I never found success in sloppiness.

Surround yourself with what you need to do your best work. That may be software programs, reference items, a mood board or just a damn comfortable chair.

[DILIGENCE]

Find a daily rhythm that works for you and your creative partner. Map out your day and block out your calendar.

Treat your creative time as sacred, not something you'll get to in between meetings and phone calls.

Close your door, silence your phone. Block out the rest of the world for an hour or two and really focus on the work at hand.

And, by all means, clean your brushes.

FIRST LINE OF DEFENSE

Coming up with great ideas is tough. Keeping them alive and intact is sometimes tougher.

From concept approval through final execution, ideas are forced to run a gauntlet of opinions—poked, prodded, gnawed and occasionally mauled by well-meaning clients.

If an idea makes it to the finish line without being dismembered, it's a small miracle.

Ironically, the first and sometimes best line of defense isn't you, but your account executive. Which is why working with great account people is critical.

Somewhere in these pages, you'll hear me rail on some of my account brethren. Guilty as charged. I have zero patience for bad ones.

But the good ones? The smart, battle-tested, client whisperers? I would go to war with them any day.

Account executives live in the trenches. They're constantly on client calls, in meetings and often asked about the creative when the creative folks aren't in earshot.

A good account person knows that every client suggestion isn't a mandate. They can douse small flames before wildfires spread. They know when to take a bullet and when

[DILIGENCE]

to fire one. And sometimes, the best defense is just "let us get back to you on that."

Not all account folks are genetically-wired to protect the work. Many haven't worked in great creative agencies.

But if you grow up in a shop whose reputation is built on its creative product, you learn how to protect the work at every turn.

Great account executives have mastered the art of respectfully pushing back. They build trust and put clients at ease.

They don't just manage clients, they lead them.

Find an account partner with a deep reverence for the creative work and you can move mountains together.

LOST IN TRANSLATION

Okay, let's just say it: writing good dialogue is hard.

Damn hard.

It shouldn't be, right? It's something we do every day. Conversations are all around us.

In grocery lines, on TV, in office hallways. It's everywhere. You'd think it would be second nature to write.

The craft of putting words in someone else's mouth, however, is tough. It often comes out clunky, morbidly stiff, and artificial.

Maybe I'm simply not a gifted dialogue writer, but I can count on one hand the number of writers I know who truly are. They've probably all moved on to writing sitcoms or screenplays because they can.

When I'm concepting a commercial or video, I try to resist the siren call of dialogue altogether.

Instead, I look for settings or situations that play out visually. Let the audience observe, connect the dots on their own.

Maybe there's a short VO line that wraps up the idea. Or, God forbid, a small scrap of dialogue to put a bow on it.

[DILIGENCE]

Visuals communicate quickly. They speak a universal language—nothing lost in translation.

Dialogue, on the other hand, does not move quickly. It bogs down and chews up time. When you're working inside a 30-second time slot or even a two-minute video, there's not a lot of time for "and then he said, and then she said."

So when in doubt, zip it. Show, don't tell. For me, less is always more.

HEADLINES AND HAND GRENADES

Oddly enough, these two share a common trait: Timing.

A great headline doesn't slap you across the face. It draws you in. It whispers, intrigues you. Nudges and invites you to think for a second.

Great headlines give the reader the satisfaction of connecting the dots, *Oh yeah, I get it.*

That's their reward. A chance to use their brain and feel better for it.

The best lines work a lot like hand grenades. They don't explode on contact. They land, neurons start sparking inside the reader's mind. Tick, tick, tick—BOOM!

This all happens in a matter of microseconds.

Timing is the trick. Too few ticks and it's too obvious. Too many ticks and your reader bails. Mere ticks are the difference between an unforgettable thought or an overcomplicated dud.

I've seen it happen dozens of times when presenting lines. The client thinks for a beat, the wheels turn for a split second, then a smile breaks from ear to ear.

BOOM! Contact.

[DILIGENCE]

Words need to be sifted through. You don't just pick them, you pan for them. Swirl the pan, sift the grit, keep the gold.

When describing someone, are they simply shy? Or are they withdrawn? Introverted? Standoffish? Skittish?

Each word choice brings a slightly different visual to mind. Tear through your thesaurus like it owes you money.

Headlines are crafted word by word.

Once you're convinced your line has found its perfect form, pull the pin.

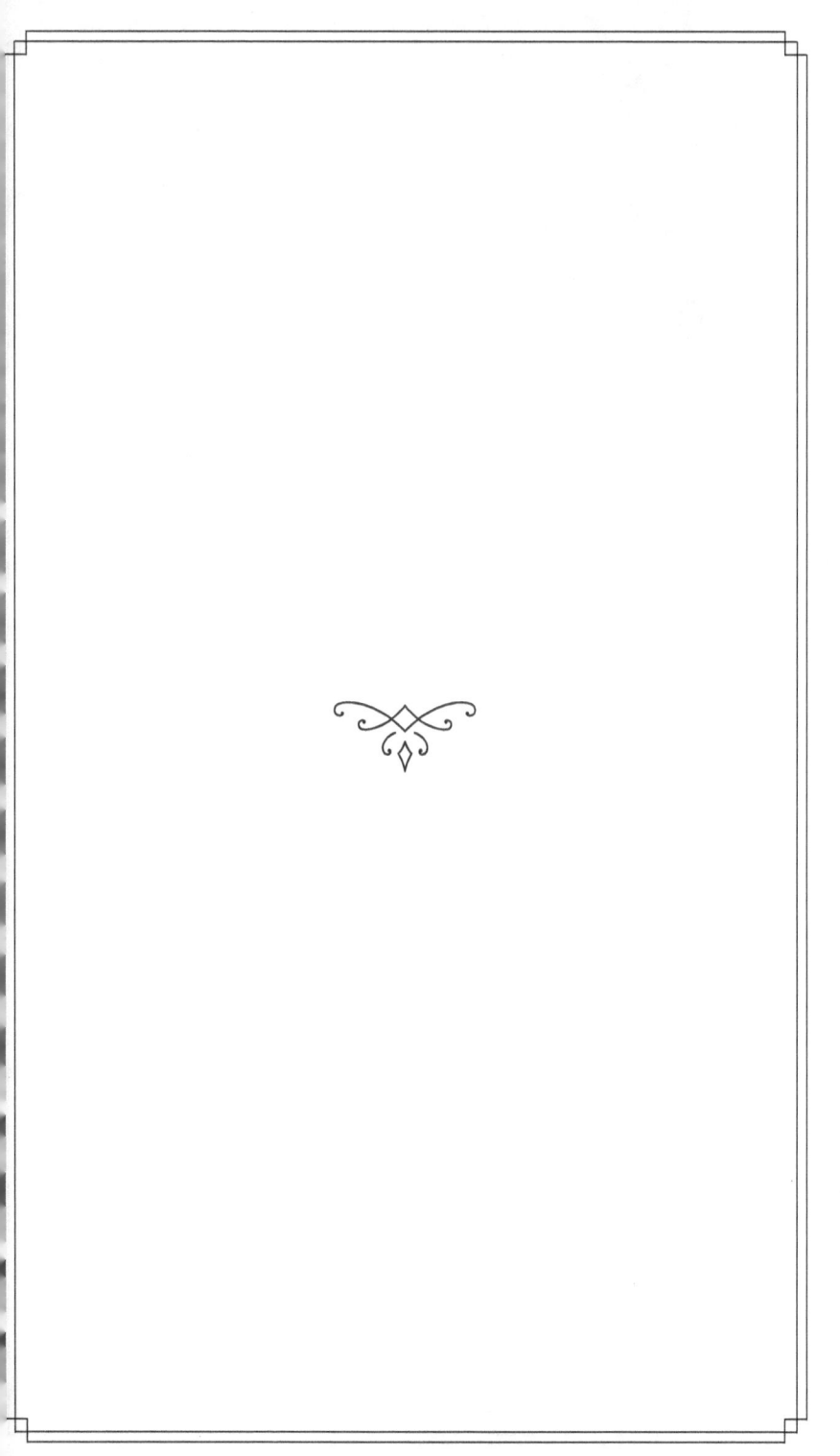

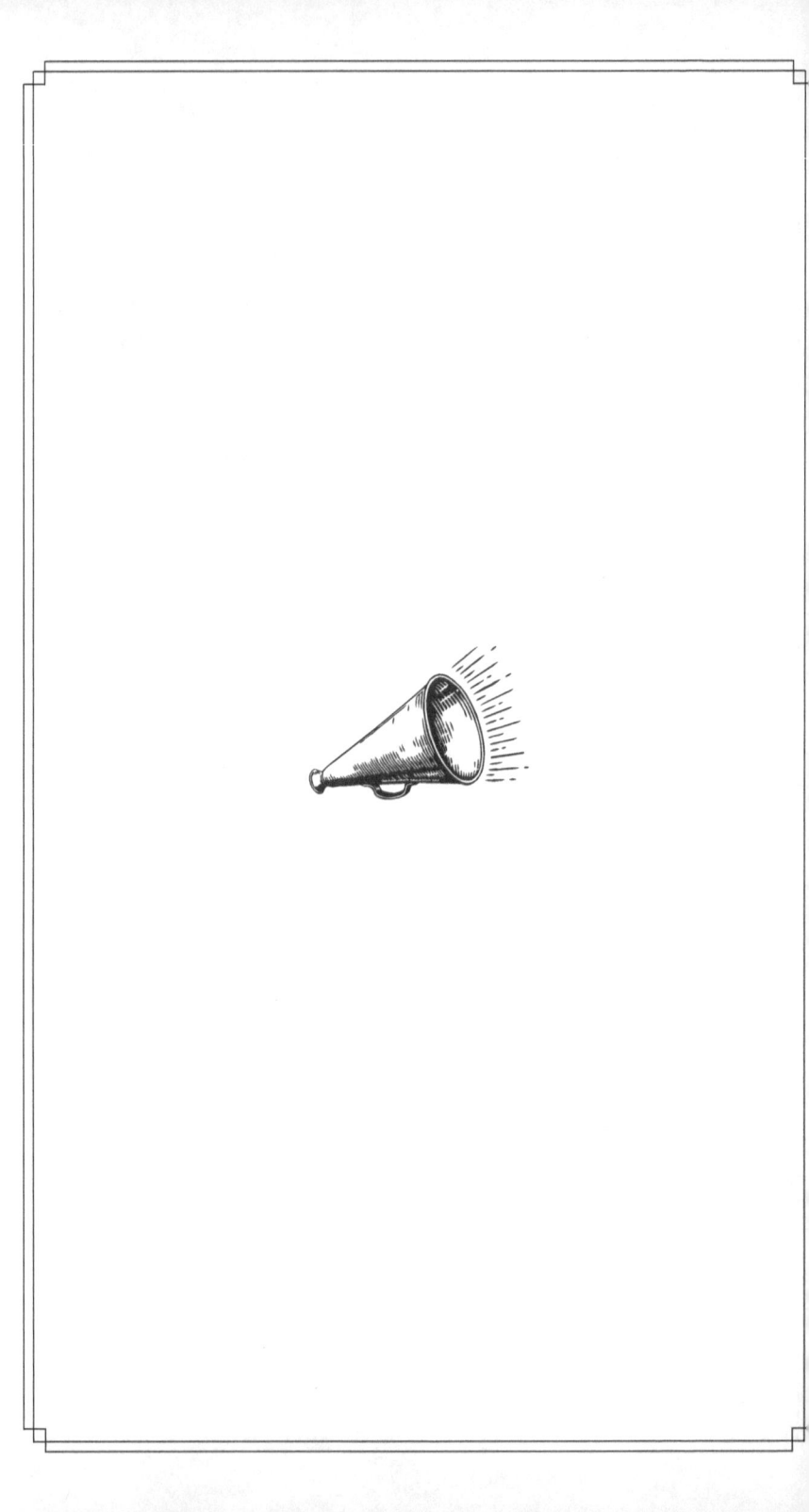

Step 3

AMBITION

Talent alone will not make you a star.

No interest in being a star? Consider digging ditches.

Just as grueling, but done in anonymity.

NO ROOM FOR WALLFLOWERS

You may be sitting in your portfolio school classroom right now, your newly-awarded Senior Copywriter's office, or perhaps, your Chief Creative Officer's corner suite.

Regardless of where you sit in the creative food chain, know this: sharks are circling.

And that's a good thing.

Creative competition isn't something to fear. It's the best performance-enhancing drug around.

Competition pushes and fuels us. It makes us better—and everyone around us.

Just like championship teams, the best creative shops are built on healthy competition. Talented creatives looking to scratch and claw their way up the depth chart, one big idea at a time.

We care, we believe, and we compete because we want to be better. We want to win. And when we lose, it should hurt.

Competition is a great elixir because it builds confidence, but also, humility.

Competition can take many forms. On an individual level, we want to put ideas on the wall that make creative comrades

[AMBITION]

think, *Damn, I wish I'd come up with that.*

I've worked at agencies overrun with writers and art directors far more talented than myself.

There were great ideas everywhere you turned and it motivated all of us to dig deep and crank it up a notch.

Try to separate ourselves from the pack.

Participation awards are of little value in this field.

SPEAKING IN TONGUES

Every writer has a voice.

For most of us, it takes time to discover and many more years to craft.

I learned to concept and write ads by watching others. Masters who made the craft look effortless.

Tom McElligott's work for Porsche, with headlines like "*Fire the Chauffeur*" and "*One ride and you'll understand why most rocket scientists are German*," opened my eyes to how to engage people's brains.

Ernie Schenck's writing for The Dunham Company—boots that didn't care about luxury, polish or pretense. Ernie's words captured the raw, unadorned work ethic born into each and every boot.

Finding your voice comes from studying the voices that make you stop and take note. You borrow. You imitate. You stumble. And somewhere along the way, you begin to sound like you.

The award show annuals are a good place to start, but don't stop there.

The first time I opened Rick Bragg's novel *All Over But the Shoutin,'* I heard a voice that gave me goosebumps.

[AMBITION]

Descriptive, emotional, and cinematic, it painted scenes that twisted and turned like colors in a kaleidoscope.

The dead waved from the ditches in Korea. The arms of the soldiers reached out from bodies half in, half out of the frozen mud, as if begging for help even after their hearts had cooled and the ice had glazed their eyes. They had been shot to rags by machine guns and frozen by a subzero wind, leaving olive-drab statues in the killing, numbing cold in the mountains in the north.

Rick's words helped me understand how to harness one's imagination. How to grab your audience in a way that doesn't make them want to let go.

Find those voices who make you stop and listen. Find out why. Then find your own voice.

RAISING EXPECTATIONS

Early in my creative career, a mentor told me, "Focus on the work and the money will follow."

If you forget everything you read in these pages, remember these four words: *don't chase the money.*

The most valuable thing you have is the work in your portfolio. In fact, as a creative, it's the only thing you have. Your portfolio needs to be nurtured and fed throughout your career.

Consider this scenario: You're five years into your career. You've pocketed a handful of awards and you're making a little name for yourself. Heck, even your teeth look whiter. Maybe it's time to seek greener pastures.

What is your portfolio worth? That depends on who you ask.

Two different headhunters. One says a small, but formative West Coast shop needs a senior writer. They're offering you a nice jump in pay, but nothing earth-shattering. They don't have the deep pockets of some other shops, but their shelves are already brimming with shiny hardware. Word is, they could be the next big thing.

The other headhunter calls with a 'great opportunity' at a mega agency in New York. Their clients are household names that even your mother would recognize, but their work is crap.

[AMBITION]

Who cares? They're willing to almost double your salary.

Do you cash in? No.

Here's why this is a no-brainer. The up-and-coming West Coast agency is a shop built around delivering great creative. If you work there, your portfolio will grow and increase in value.

Meanwhile, NYC Mega is ready to serve up a straight shot of cyanide into your portfolio's veins. This is the last stop for creativity.

And while, for the short term, you may be rolling in dinero, your portfolio has officially flatlined.

Suddenly, you're upside down. Stuck in a job you can't leave. Your salary is much higher than what your portfolio is really worth.

This, my friends, is a creative death sentence.

With every career move, be thoughtful and make sure you end up at a place where you can add to and elevate your portfolio.

Your portfolio is a ticket to be cashed in at any time. The danger is cashing in too early. Don't take the bait.

HISTORY STARTS SMALL

When we launched Huey/Paprocki, our first big win wasn't big at all. The Atlanta History Center was small, local, and had only a minuscule marketing budget. But they believed great creative work could help spin the turnstiles.

That was all we needed.

Their new Marketing Director, Shawndell Hand, was young, enthusiastic and scrappy. Just like us. Her team was small, but the opportunity to grow the brand and business had everyone excited.

Little did we know, the Atlanta History Center was more than a brand—it was many brands. With new exhibits coming every month, the focus of our advertising was constantly changing.

One month, we're pushing an exhibit of 100-year-old, hand-stitched quilts. The next, diving into kids' toys from the past fifty years. Or showcasing how African dance influenced American culture.

Every new exhibit was a creative left turn. A chance to tell a new story with a new look and feel.

This was every creative's dream.

Our work for the Atlanta History Center didn't just move

[AMBITION]

ticket sales, it propelled our small agency's visibility and reputation. We were cranking out over 50 ads a year, many of which landed in the pages of *Communication Arts*, *Archive* magazine and *The One Show*.

Not bad for a "small" client.

It was also my first glimpse into how different clients serve different agency needs. What this client added to our agency's bottom line couldn't be measured in dollars and cents. But it could be measured in phone calls.

The noise this little account made grabbed the attention of larger, more lucrative clients.

Sometimes going big starts small.

SHINY THINGS

I've often heard agency heads emphatically proclaim: *awards don't matter!*

It's a convenient excuse.

Awards don't matter to the agencies incapable of winning them. So they dismiss them.

Competition is a great measuring stick. We see it in other industries. The film world has its Oscars and music has the Grammys.

Even clients want in on the action. I spent six years working on Lexus and Mercedes-Benz. Whether it was *Car & Driver's Top 10* list, *Road & Track's Performance Car of the Year*, or a slew of *J.D. Power* awards, my automotive clients always looked to leave their tire tracks.

Stuffing your shelves with shiny objects is important for a few reasons. If you're a creative looking to be hired, agencies notice.

Hardware is street cred.

If you're an agency pitching new business, clients notice. Every marketing director wants an agency with a proven record of creating work that stands out and gets noticed.

[AMBITION]

Lastly, as an agency, winning awards is a great recruiting tool. You become that agency that creatives are hellbent on breaking into.

Does award-winning work matter? Does it grow clients' business or just agency head's hat sizes?

Actually, the best creative work builds brands and their agencies with it.

A study conducted by Ipsos, a global research firm with 50 years under their belt, found that award-winning ads deliver 30 percent higher brand awareness. They are also 29 percent more effective on short-term sales and 11 percent more effective at long-term brand building.

When we deliver great work for our clients, we all reap the rewards.

A WOLF IN SHEEP'S CLOTHING

Barely a year into my first advertising job, a friend squinted at me and asked, "What are you doing working as an account executive?"

Fair question.

It's true, I was a card-carrying right-brain type. Obsessed with music, art, writing—anything that involved making stuff.

But fresh out of college, I thought the "business side" was the respectable, logical path. After all, wasn't that what a degree was for? Suits, meetings, and spreadsheets?

Two years into my account service career, I made the jump to copywriter. For years I regretted the time I spent in a starched, button-down collar with my windsor knot pulled up tight.

I convinced myself those were the "lost years." Stolen opportunities to do what I actually wanted—make ads, not PowerPoints.

But with hindsight, I realized those weren't stolen years at all. They were training wheels. A blessing in disguise.

My time as an account executive taught me how to think strategically, how to manage clients without losing my sanity, and how to keep an eye on account profitability—all skills

[AMBITION]

that later helped me start my own agency.

It's called a career path, but it's never a straight line. Not only will your journey wind, but it will dip, drop and splinter off, sometimes far from where you started out.

As long as you're taking the right turns for the right reasons, you'll land in the right spot.

SHAMELESS PROMOTION

You are a brand. And, like all brands, yours needs to be built, shaped and promoted. Your work may speak for your talent, but only if it's seen and heard. You are responsible for publicizing and building your brand.

Letting people know who you are and what you're capable of is nothing to be shy or shameful about.

This doesn't mean you need to morph into some spotlight-chasing extrovert with a bullhorn.

Carnival barkers aren't in high demand these days.

But you do need to get out there. Join in the conversation. Raise your hand. Say yes to that panel discussion. Go back and speak at your college or university. If you believe in the power of great creative, find a platform.

Exposure builds confidence.

Look for opportunities to judge award shows. And when the call comes, grab it like a golden ticket.

There are local advertising clubs scattered from Memphis to Phoenix, Charlotte to Cincinnati and everywhere in between. Right now, their ad club boards are scratching their heads and wondering, *Who can we get to speak? Who can we put on our ADDY Awards judging panel?*

[AMBITION]

They're constantly looking for names, so drop yours in their hat. Don't wait for them to find you, find them. Judging shows builds instant credibility and introduces you to other creatives out there.

As we often say, *"It's a people business."* Don't hide behind your portfolio. Let your personality shine. Be engaging. Be generous. Be known.

If you choose to live in the shadows, your career will likely dwell there as well.

WILL IT MAKE US FAMOUS?

If bright lights bother you, this may not be the stage for you. We're not here to be backup players. It's too much hard work.

In baseball, nobody dreams of batting .200. They're chasing All-Star rosters, MVP trophies, rings, parades down Main Street.

That's the league we're playing in.

As creatives, our legacy is stamped by the work itself. Is it sharper than what the agency across town is showing off? Strong enough to get people talking in other cities, on other coasts? Bold enough to generate buzz for our clients and momentum for us?

That's the question: *will it make us famous?*

This isn't vanity, it's a filter. A rallying cry. A reason to push past "good enough" and chase ideas that can't be ignored.

We all agree that mediocrity is the yellow brick road to nowhere. Invisibility. Both clients and agencies say the same thing—they want greatness.

Talent is never the problem. I'm constantly blown away by the army of creative minds out there. Every discipline, every coast, every city. Talent is not in short supply.

[AMBITION]

True, we're all capable of award-winning work. But this isn't a Home Run Derby. No one's lobbing softballs down the middle.

Conceiving and producing great work is a challenge and it can't be achieved alone.

When I think about the work I am most proud of, there was always a great client at our side. A partner with vision, guts, and skin in the game.

Talent needs opportunity.

You can't craft award-winning work without clients willing to shoot for the stars with you. They're out there—you just have to find them.

The best part is that great work will make you both famous.

FACES, NOT PLACES

It's easy to be lured by the agency or company name on the door, but once you're inside, who will you be directly working for? Who will you be learning from? Do you admire and respect their work? Do you like their style?

What is their temperament? Are they fond of throwing things? Is their reputation as a good manager or absentee boss? Get some intel.

The people you report to will shape what you learn, how you think, and how you navigate throughout your career. This is true regardless of your title or discipline.

When you're just starting out, you need a mentor and sherpa. Someone to help you navigate agency life before you splat like a baby bird kicked too early from the nest.

Fast-forward a few years. You have a handful of hardware to show for your toils. A little swagger in your step. Maybe there's an ACD position in your future. Is your new Creative Director going to give you some autonomy or make you just their finger puppet?

The point is: bosses matter a lot.

Remember, you're interviewing the agency and their people as much as they're interviewing you. Choose wisely.

[AMBITION]

Agency size matters. In small agencies, culture is everything. Teams are small and closely-knit. You won't have to look far to figure out who'll be reviewing your work, which clients you'll be working with, and how well-stocked the breakroom is.

Large agencies can be a mixed bag. The way one account is run can be very different from the next depending on who's steering the ship. The creative work can vary from group to group.

Big or small, marquee name or hidden gem, the people who guide, shape, and approve your work will define your success more than any logo on the door.

So do your homework. Ask around.

In this business, who you work for often matters just as much as where you work.

HANGING OUT SHINGLES

Starting your own agency (or any business) is incredibly exciting and horribly terrifying at the same time.

When my partner, Joe, and I opened Huey/Paprocki, I'd just turned 37 with two-week-old twins, Nicholas and Alex. Needless to say, my head was spinning.

If you're the type who will always wonder, *"What if?",* my advice is simple: take the plunge.

Running your own shop means being ready for a lot more than just creative work. Suddenly, you're juggling things you never signed up for: business licenses, payroll, landlords, leases, office build-outs, furnishings, constant new business chasing, and quarterly tax payments.

Fun, right?

Actually, once you get past the business part of the business, it can be very rewarding. Maybe for this reason only: You are your own boss. You answer to no one. No hack Creative Director killing your ideas. No holding company scrutinizing your profit margins. No agency presidents demanding to pitch the massive telecom account with the horrible reputation.

Nothing is more freeing than the ability to make your own decisions. And you'll have plenty to make.

[AMBITION]

Joe and I were lucky because we knew our agency's edge would be the creative work. That north star became our calling card and attracted like-minded clients.

Yes, we were all in on the creative work. But focusing on the work and ignoring the finances is the shortest route to the unemployment line. So we watched every expense, stayed lean and never overextended ourselves. Low overhead allowed us to keep our creative standards high and be picky about the clients we brought on.

Running your own agency will test your principles, your patience and occasionally, your sanity. But if you have the opportunity to start your own place, or become a partner, it can be the adventure of a lifetime.

The best part? If it doesn't work out, you can always go back to your day job: Working for someone else. No shame in that. No judgment. Just a little wiser and a lot bolder.

Step 4

TRUST

This is not a solo mission.

Build bonds with those in your foxhole.

When the bullets start flying,

trust is your strongest ally.

CATS AND DOGS

Creatives and account folks often butt heads. We're just different breeds, often with different objectives.

As stereotypes go, creatives can be aloof and known to hiss, scratch and claw in defense of the work. Account types are generally more peaceful and accommodating.

A lovable labrador aiming to please.

But anywhere you find great work being done, you'll find these two opposites not only happily cohabitating, but constantly collaborating.

You need both perspectives and skills to foster great work.

You need the team.

It's okay that creatives are looking to line their shelves with work that stands out. Exceptional work builds brands and agencies.

Meanwhile, account folks have more to juggle than just creative needs. Including account profitability, marshalling agency resources and client wrangling. And often, just trying to keep the peace.

Working on the Mercedes-Benz business, I was fortunate to work with an amazing account team in Greg Zuercher and

[TRUST]

Roger Ferguson. They understood that stellar creative work was why the client came to us and what the agency was built on. Having that clear, shared purpose grounded our relationship.

When we reviewed concepts with Greg and Roger, they were most often very excited and supportive. They trusted our creative group to do what we do.

Yet, the few times they raised concerns and spoke up, we were all ears. They knew the client and understood where the land mines were hidden. When their radar went up, ours did, too.

Our different perspectives made us a stronger team.

Given that type of trust and mutual respect, rarely did the fur fly.

A CONFESSION

Dick Lyons, our client at Mizuno, was one of the good ones. Smart, honest and trusting. Dick knew golf clubs inside and out: loft, lie, grooves, shaft flex, you name it.

But he also knew creativity wasn't his thing. That's why he hired us.

One day, when briefing us on Mizuno's new MP-62 irons, Dick went down the technological rabbit hole, explaining all the intricate improvements: a lower center of gravity, variable face thickness, increased launch angle.

My head was spinning like a duck hook off the first tee.

I finally stopped him and asked, "Dick, in layman's terms, what does it do?"

Dick stared at the ceiling, thought for a moment and succinctly replied, "It's like you never hit a bad shot. Hit it on the toe, on the heel—the ball still flies straight. It's almost like you're cheating."

There it was. The line, the truth, the insight—all neatly teed up for us.

We came back a week or two later with an image showing a dozen golfers, decked out in golf shirts and khakis, standing in a confessional line inside a cathedral.

[TRUST]

The small inset visual featured a beauty shot of the MP-62 iron with the headline: *You'll feel like you're cheating*.

Before we presented it, I opened with, "Dick, remember when you mentioned cheating? Well, that got us thinking." Seeing the concept, Dick's face lit up. He could see his words come to life and that gave him ownership in the idea.

When clients see their fingerprints on the work, they're invested. It's no longer your idea, it's our idea.

Now your chances of producing something great go up exponentially.

Sometimes the best concepts come from just taking the time to listen. You never know when the client might drop the idea right in your lap.

YOU'RE MY SHINING STAR

When our clients win, we win. It's that simple.

Marketing directors want to be heroes within their own company walls just like we want to shine as agency stars.

But it's not just about giving them great ideas, it's about arming them with the insights, rationale, and ammo they may need to sell it up the chain.

Too often, we kill the initial presentation, trading high fives in the parking lot afterwards. Only to hear, a week later, that the CEO wasn't feeling it and it's back to the drawing board.

This is a shame. Mainly, because it may have been avoidable. Too often ideas aren't given the right context and proper setup. Things fall between the cracks and are easily lost in translation.

Not all marketing directors are natural-born presenters. Some struggle to communicate the magic you've crafted. This is understandable and why they're not in your shoes.

The best-case scenario is to find a way to be included when your client presents the concepts up the chain.

Good marketing directors often welcome this because they know that performing on the big stage is what we do. We're an extension of their team and make them look good.

[TRUST]

Presenting creative ideas is what we're trained for. It's our circus act. I don't care if I look like a juggling monkey. Give me the chance to present our ideas in their best light.

If I can't sell them through, then that's on me and I can live with that.

When you make your clients look good to their bosses, trust grows. Loyalty grows. And most importantly, you become indispensable.

That's a pretty great place to be.

GUT INSTINCTS

Make no doubt about it, creatives are artists. We paint with words and pictures. Each of us puts our unique touch on our work.

That often means making tough decisions, sometimes on the fly. Especially when concepts move into execution.

Sorting through hundreds of actor head shots, dozens of voiceover auditions, music choices, wardrobe options and shoot locations can turn into mental quicksand.

You're making tough, but critical decisions here. Often, staring down the barrel of tight timelines.

Prep like you're studying for a final exam. Go in knowing what you're looking for. And what you're not.

With talent auditions, if you don't see or hear it in the first five seconds, say "no" and move on. Don't overthink it. Trust your gut.

Choosing commercial directors can be tricky as well. Is their vision in line with yours? Do they see what you see?

We were faced with an interesting situation when reviewing directors for an upcoming Lexus shoot.

Michael Grasso, a very accomplished director, had never

[TRUST]

shot a car commercial. His reel had some really nice work, including some heartfelt 7-Eleven spots, but not a glint of sheet metal anywhere in sight.

Still, when we discussed the concept with him, his take lined up perfectly with ours.

Choosing a 'non-car' director for a Lexus shoot raised a few eyebrows. Okay, maybe a few dozen. But our client trusted our instincts and agreed to the unconventional choice.

The result was one of the most memorable commercials the brand ever produced: the Lexus LS400 gracefully gliding across a frozen lake to show off its traction control system.

Nothing on Michael's reel said he was "the guy." But our gut said otherwise.

Creativity isn't always about the safest choice, but the smartest risk. The one that feels right in your bones, even when the data disagrees. Sometimes that gamble pays off in gold.

Or in this case, ice.

CHEMISTRY WINS

This is a game of ideas, right?

Early in my career, I believed that. I thought that the best and brightest ideas would always rise to the top. I assumed that brilliance was self-evident. Undeniable.

In new business pitches, I was convinced that the smartest, boldest, most original thinking would win the day.

After all, isn't the idea the holy grail?

Not always.

Here's what they don't teach you in advertising school: there are lots of great agencies out there with lots of great work.

Let's say you're a client looking for an agency with creative horsepower. You throw a party and invite Wieden+Kennedy, Goodby Silverstein & Partners, The Martin Agency, 72andSunny and Chiat/Day.

Here's one thing I can promise you: The room's going to be wallpapered with killer thinking. You could close your eyes, toss a dart, and hit something smart.

When the work can't separate agencies, chemistry does.

Clients don't just buy ideas, they buy the people behind

[TRUST]

them. The best creative concepts in the world won't save you if the client doesn't like you, doesn't trust you, or can't picture sitting next to you on a cross-country flight.

Great chemistry is the first step to great creative work. When clients like you and believe in you, they'll take giant leaps. They'll defend your work when you're not in the room. And they'll buy bolder, more unexpected ideas, faster.

Chemistry leads to confidence. And confidence brings creative opportunity.

OPEN BOOKS

I'm not good at hiding things. Which makes me a terrible poker player, but has served me well with clients and team members through the years.

Transparency builds trust.

As a creative director, you need clients who trust your instincts and guidance. Your chances of selling great work often hinges on the client's belief that you have their brand interests at heart, not yours.

You also need creative teams who know you have their backs. On this front, your actions will speak louder than your words.

Give your creatives a chance to solve the problem without solving it for them. Give them direction, not mandates.

The line between being a creative director and a creative dictator is a fine one.

Your job as a creative director isn't to do the work, but cultivate it and polish it.

Hire talented creatives and give them the chance to shine even when the client is slinging curveballs. Protect and nurture them at every turn. That builds loyalty with your teams, and in turn, grows your legacy and reputation.

[TRUST]

As an agency owner, be proactive with clients. Keep them in the loop on everything—not just creative. Keep them up to date with invoicing, estimated production costs, agency time, anything that might blindside them.

Clients appreciate when you're one step ahead of every question.

When you're open and honest, trust follows. And trust can erase doubt faster than a Tide stick.

LUNCH DATES

If the only time you see your client is across a conference room table, or worse, in a tiny pixelated square on Google Meet, you're doing it all wrong.

Relationships aren't built over PowerPoint decks, ROI charts and creative timelines. To produce good creative work, you need bonding moments.

So get out of the office. Close the laptop. Find ways to spend time with your clients when work isn't the topic. Lunch is easy. Ballgames. Concerts. Happy hours.

Anywhere far away from the land of bad coffee and the numbing buzz of fluorescent lighting. This is your chance to talk about anything and everything but work.

Ask about their kids, their hobbies, their aging dog or recent move. Those small, personal moments are where trust is earned.

When you get to know someone as a person, labels like client and agency partner start to fall away. Trust steps in.

We all hate being called a "Vendor." If you don't want to be treated like one, work harder at being a friend. A confidante. Be curious. Thoughtful. Show up like a human being who actually cares about life more than work.

[TRUST]

Over the years, I've made it a habit to ask my clients about their families and interests outside of work. Not because it's polite, but because it matters. People notice when you treat them as more than an income stream.

I get it. Not every client is someone you want to chug a beer with. Understood. But you can still find common ground. A shared laugh. A good story. Something meaningful.

The better you know your client, the more they trust you. That's when creative walls crumble and the opportunity for bold thinking emerges.

When we talk about knowing your audience, it also means knowing your client. So make a lunch date. Put it on the calendar. And don't forget to pick up the tab.

CIRCLE OF TRUST

Advertising is a big, wide world filled with street corner pushers, self-proclaimed saints and profit prophets.

Opinions are currency.

Figuring out who to listen to and who to trust can be tricky, but it's incredibly important.

Find your people—a small circle of friends who will undoubtedly shoot you straight. The ones who will tell you your 'brilliant idea' is just okay. Or that job you're considering is at an agency that chews up creatives and spits them out. The ones who will tell you the truth—even when it stings a bit.

Firsthand relationships can help avoid a lot of second-guessing.

Five years into running my own agency, I was still emailing rough concepts to my old creative partners asking: Is this any good? Does this make any sense? Am I a total hack?

Over the years, my little network has saved me countless times. From creative misfires to client meltdowns to avoiding bad landlords.

Your circle of trust can be your lifeline in this business. Choose wisely. Keep it small.

[TRUST]

This doesn't have to be a collection of ad folks. In fact, outside perspectives may be even more valuable. Be curious. Don't be afraid to peel back the curtain and ask tough questions.

Friends want to help. In fact, they're there to help.

The ad world is filled with voices. Many claiming to know all the answers, shouting above the crowd. Circle your wagons. Tune out the rest of the noise.

It's not always who you listen to, but who you don't.

RESEARCH PROVES RESEARCH WORKS

My friend, Ken Lewis, once wrote that headline for an Atlanta Ad Club campaign and I still laugh to this day. Because it's true. And not true. All at once.

Market research is a powerful weapon. But in the wrong hands, it's a molotov cocktail ready to spray death and fiery destruction across every bold, beautiful idea on the creative battlefield.

Don't get me wrong. I like numbers as much as the next data jockey. I can even appreciate a brightly-colored bar graph or an occasional pie chart.

The problem is the numbers don't always add up.

They tend to squeeze out any hint of bravery, imagination and unconventional thinking. The bigger problem is that many clients are prone to 'trust the numbers' because it's their SVP-of-Marketing's-ass on the line.

Let's use research for good.

Research can point us to the right audiences and measure market opportunity. It can give us great insight into what motivates people and can help feed creativity. What we learn from research on the front end can make our ideas smarter, sharper and more relevant on the back end.

[TRUST]

What research can't do is measure magic. It can't put a number on ingenuity and creative impact.

The minute someone is asked what they think about a creative concept, emotions leave the room. Gut reactions disappear. They're taken out of the real world and ushered into the world of intellectual pontification.

People want to look and sound smart. Observations like, *"I love it, it made me laugh"* seem too simple, too superficial. So instead we get responses like *"Hmmm… I'm not sure the strategic pillars are aligning with the demographic profiles."*

When data turns people into dots on a matrix, their hearts stop beating. We lose touch. Instead of consumers, we're trying to communicate with spreadsheets and personas.

So yes, research proves that research works. Just don't let it prove your ideas don't.

COMFORT ZONES

There is comfort in the familiar. What we know. What we've seen. What we've experienced before.

But in advertising, familiarity is a trap door. Ready and waiting to drop you into the dark abyss of mediocrity.

Creatively, it's easy to fall back on the expected routes. We can do that in our sleep.

But traveling a well-worn path is only going to lead you to creative dead ends. When you should be hacking through the jungle with a machete of originality.

Most clients aren't ready to buckle up for a rocky ride into uncharted territory. They're trained to love the data, trust the charts and cling to the comfort of the predictable and proven.

I've been fortunate to work with a handful of brave clients. Clients eager to break new ground and shatter old rules.

One the best is Melissa Floyd, Chief Marketing & Communications Officer at Stryten Energy. Over the years, we've built great trust with Melissa and her team and they've learned to expect the unexpected from us.

Stryten builds premium automotive batteries that last up to three times longer than conventional ones. For a recent

[TRUST]

campaign, we figured who better to convey the virtues of battery life … and death, than the Grim Reaper himself.

Death as a spokesperson isn't something most clients sign up for.

Melissa did.

Weeks after presenting the campaign and well into production, Melissa pulled me aside and said, "I knew the Grim Reaper was a big idea because it made me uncomfortable."

As a creative, you can't ask for more than that.

To produce great work, you have to shake off the familiar. Step out of your comfort zone. And have a client that's willing to take the leap with you.

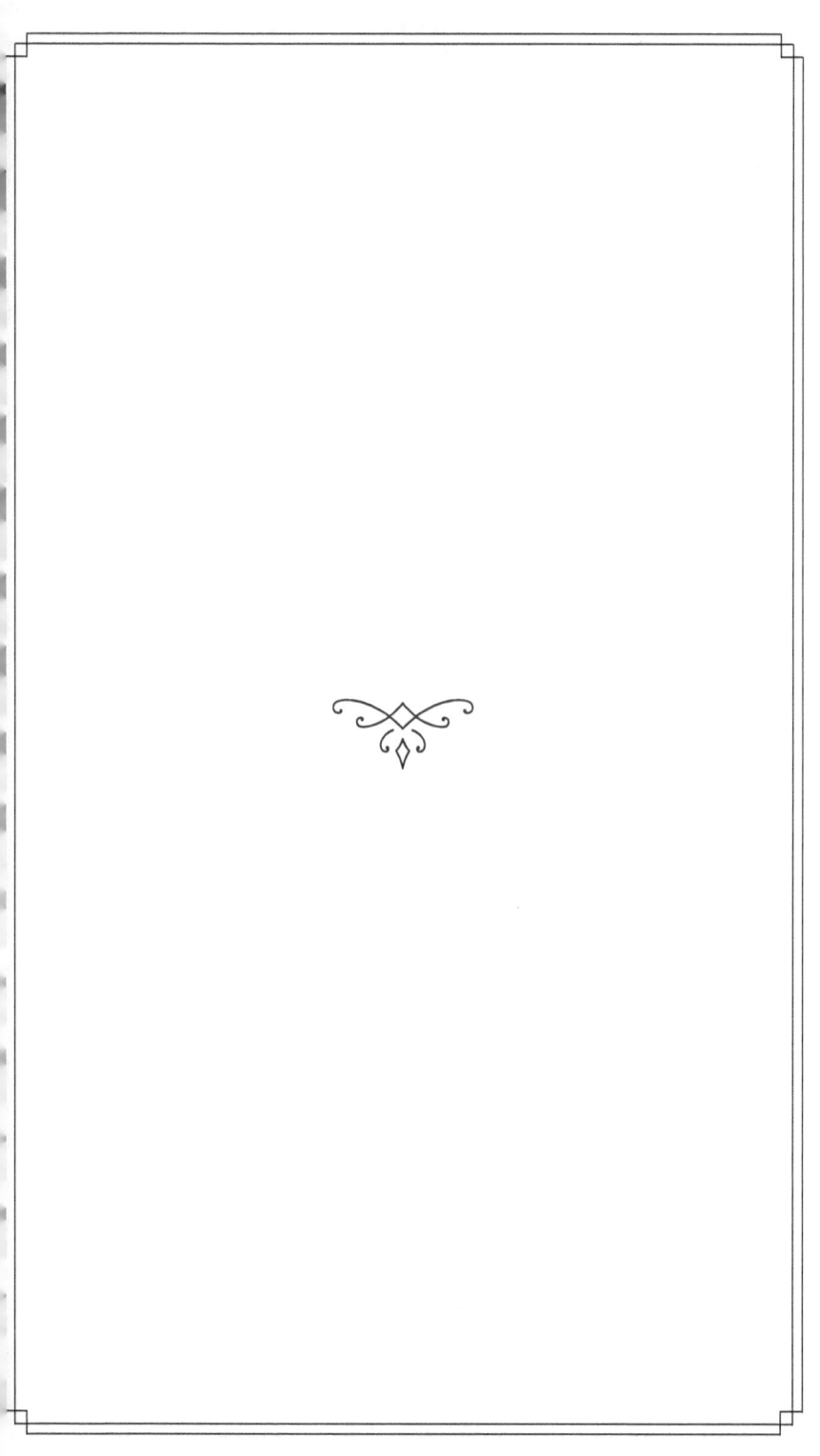

Step 5

HUMILITY

It's easy to let success go to your head. But remember, you're only an assignment away from being brought to your knees.

SUCCESS IS FLEETING

As creatives, we're groomed to carry confidence like a well-curated accessory, brimming with style and substance.

If we don't believe in ourselves and our ideas, who will?

Yet some of the most decorated creative minds in our business, including Jerry Cronin, Luke Sullivan, Dean Buckhorn and Steve Bassett, are some of the most humble people you could ever meet.

It's not because they lack talent. It would take a fleet of dump trucks to haul away the hardware they've won.

They simply know that success is not a permanent state. Instead, just a temporary achievement. They know the ice is slick and the floor is hard.

Great creative minds share a common fear that the next time they are faced with a blank canvas, they'll do an epic faceplant.

Exposed as hacks, frauds and has-beens.

It's why the best, most accomplished creatives don't live off their successes, but feed off their failures. They know defeat is just a creative brief away.

It's a healthy way to think.

[HUMILITY]

I wouldn't call it imposter syndrome. That's too harsh. This isn't about doubt, but determination. The need to prove yourself again.

It's a well-earned respect for how the creative process works. The reality that wins come with losses. There's always room for improvement.

Celebrate your victories, but count them later.

The opportunity is straight ahead. Stay focused on the next assignment, the next challenge.

Tennis great, Roger Federer, won 20 Grand Slam titles. But he won them one game at a time.

There will be time for looking back. Use the fear of failure as a healthy way to keep pushing forward.

FIRST CLASS MISTAKES

Travel is hard-coded into our business. Production shoots. Out of town clients. Trade shows. Factory tours. Sales meetings. Frequent flyer miles aplenty.

It's exciting for sure, but it can wear on you. A couple of late client dinners and suddenly room service and SportsCenter on the laptop sound mighty appealing.

We'd just wrapped up a presentation to the West Coast Mercedes-Benz dealers at a nondescript hotel on the outskirts of LAX.

Our small group, including our agency president, John Adams, was due to fly back to Richmond.

John was a lanky, towering gentleman with feet the size of small boat oars. He was welcoming and easy to get to know, with a mind sharper than a radial saw.

It was a five-hour, cross-country trip and we all had our fingers crossed to be upgraded to first class.

My golden ticket came in and I was granted a spacious lair in the first few rows of the plane. My oversized seat practically swallowed my 160-pound frame.

Lucky me.

[HUMILITY]

An hour into the flight, I headed toward the back of the plane to the restroom. Somewhere around row 35, I found our president, John Adams.

He was folded into a narrow economy seat, knees under his chin and head pressed against the wall of the fuselage. He mustered a tired smile for me.

John did not deserve this. Agency presidents aren't meant for coach class. Yet, even with his lofty title, he showed amazing grace.

Now, years later, I realize how selfish and stupid I was. I should have insisted John take my first-class seat.

I should have known my place and been mature enough to make the right call. I should have shown some respect.

Our reputations are built by our actions. The choices we make. The impressions we leave.

I could have demonstrated a little class.

TWO-WAY STREETS

Route 82 is a narrow, two-lane stretch of asphalt that weaves between open pastures, over the Middle Oconee River and past small, wooden churches with paint peeling from the blistering Georgia summers.

It's a short, peaceful 10-mile drive that connects the towns of Winder and Statham.

I grew up in Winder, just a dot on the map about an hour northeast of Atlanta. My best friend, Russell Newton, lived in Statham, an even smaller speck of a town.

Once we were old enough to drive, I'd chide Russell to fire up his Dodge Colt and make the short drive into Winder. He was happy to oblige. After all, Winder was where the action was, a few downtown shops, a McDonald's, and more stop lights than you could count on one hand.

After a summer full of trips into Winder, I called Russell early one Saturday morning asking what time I should expect him.

His response caught me off guard: "You know that road runs both ways."

So true.

Advertising is, indeed, a two-way street. Give and take is essential.

[HUMILITY]

Don't expect things to always go your way. You won't win every creative battle, so choose them carefully. Some ideas aren't a hill worth dying on. Save your powder for more important issues.

Communication with clients and within the agency should also run both ways. Be respectful. Don't turn dialogues into monologues. Every voice deserves to be heard. When you prevent that from happening, you lose credibility.

Before you mandate 'my way or the highway,' remember that, in advertising, one-way streets often lead to dead ends.

TAILS BETWEEN LEGS

Late one Friday afternoon, as work was wrapping up and happy hour cocktails were already being served, the account executive on Wrangler Jeans stepped cautiously into my office.

Apparently, our Wrangler client was still not happy with my third attempt at their minuscule copy printed on the garment hangtag.

I was clearly over this little project when Mike Hughes, my boss and agency creative director, walked in. Mike sensed my frustration and that I somehow felt this task was beneath me, especially late on a Friday afternoon.

Wasn't this a job for a junior copywriter, not an agency VP?

Measuring the desperation in the account executive's eyes, Mike calmly offered, "I can revise the hangtag copy tonight."

What?

My cowboy-sized ego quickly shrank to field mouse-sized proportions.

When the blood returned to my head, I gulped, turned to Mike and explained that I'd be happy to take another stab at the copy over the weekend.

[HUMILITY]

Then I crawled back into my mouse hole.

If the creative leader of our 250+ person agency was willing to write the hangtag copy on his Friday night, who was I to refuse? Even with Mike's lofty title, he was clearly not above the task at hand. That's leadership.

He was looking to solve a problem, not complain about one.

There will be creative tasks that seem inconsequential. Something that can be put off, handed off, just make it go away.

But if it matters to your client, it should matter to you.

CULTURE CLUB

When you rise to the ranks of Creative Director, you're faced with the challenge of not actually doing the work, but managing, cultivating and shaping the work.

And with that, the people behind it.

Creative directors are like coaches. You're only as good as your players. How do you bring out the best in them?

At The Martin Agency, I was fortunate to work with a stable of young, creative talent including Tripp Westbrook, Mark Wenneker, Jeff Ross, Jonathan Mackler, Anne-Marie Hite, Scott Stripling, Tony Bennett and many others. But even with a stacked line-up, our creative department still needed a few more ringers.

That's when a five-star portfolio slid across my desk. A young kid right out of the Creative Circus. Let's call him Chuck.

Chuck's work wasn't like other ad school books, the ideas jumped off the page and I liked what I saw. We couldn't get him on a plane to Richmond fast enough.

As Chuck sat across from me, he confidently guided me through his work. Pointing out his thinking along the way.

What struck me was that Chuck never mentioned his creative partners.

[HUMILITY]

Or how fortunate he was to attend a school like the Creative Circus.

No kind words about the teachers who, without their efforts, he wouldn't be sitting here.

Chuck never once noted our agency's work, what he loved or how and why he would be a great fit.

I saw pounds of great thinking, but not an ounce of humility. For me, that was a big red flag.

I thanked Chuck for his time, wished him luck and made sure his travel arrangements home were in order.

When it's time to hire, think about who you're bringing into your little tight-knit community. You need more than great thinkers, you need great fits.

Skills can be taught and shaped, but personality traits are usually hard-wired in.

I wonder what ever happened to ol' Chucky boy?

DIRTY DISHES

Being a "highly-decorated creative" doesn't excuse you from picking up after yourself. You're not royalty. You're a team member.

It doesn't hurt to straighten conference room chairs when you leave a meeting. Wipe down the counter when you spill coffee. Act like you own the place—because if you did, you'd definitely care.

Let your reputation speak for more than just bright ideas.

Running my own agency taught me plenty about cultivating great creative work. But it also taught me that peace lilies are thirstier than interns, that "antique white" actually comes in 47 different shades of beige, and that a plate of day-old spaghetti turns into cement overnight—unless you let it soak.

Take pride in your work, but also take pride in your workplace. It is a reflection of who you are, how you run your business.

Is it clean, neat and in order? Or does it look more like a frat house on an early Sunday morning?

Part of a leader's job is to manage the ship. Even down to the smallest detail. It's the little stuff that speaks to who you really are.

[HUMILITY]

Whether you're a creative director, a fresh hire or somewhere in between, roll up your sleeves. Scrub the mug. Clear the table. Earn your stripes—not just with ideas, but with action.

In the end, it's not about dirty dishes. It's about humility and respect.

TYRANTS

There are some incredibly talented and accomplished creatives in our business who have climbed to the highest rung of their companies by being complete monsters.

Full of talent and full of themselves. The reason they're not fired is because they're really, really good at coming up with great ideas.

No matter how talented these bullies are, avoid them.

Toxic creative directors keep everyone on edge because you never know quite when they're going to go off like a roman candle.

Implode. Explode. Yell things, throw things.

Many creative directors are infamous for dressing down account people, belittling their creative team members, or even pushing back on clients until all eyes in the room are nervously scanning for the exit.

I've found that intimidation, humiliation, and verbal threats aren't good teachers or motivators. There's a difference between tough love and outright abuse.

Tell me my ideas suck. But I don't need it yelled at me or digitally wadded up and hurled in my direction.

[HUMILITY]

Mike Hughes, whom I mention often, helped build one of the country's hottest creative shops from Richmond, Virginia, of all places.

Presenting creative work to Mike was always difficult. He was a legend, but a quiet one. Mike never felt like he had to scold, challenge, or belittle you. You were an adult.

When Mike liked your work, it was immediate and his mammoth frame would light up. When your ideas weren't met with his immediate enthusiasm, nothing needed saying. The disappointed look in Mike's eyes was motivating enough.

This business is tough enough. Work with people you admire and respect.

Life is too short to work with tyrants.

BROTHER, MY BROTHER

This business has a way of inflating egos faster than a hot-air balloon at Coachella. A few shiny awards, a little success tucked under your Burberry belt, and suddenly we're strutting around like we invented advertising.

Here's a truth I've always liked:

"You can easily judge the character of a man by how he treats those who can do nothing for him." —Johann Wolfgang von Goethe

Goethe was a poet, playwright, scientist and critic. Basically, the original overachiever. And even back in the 1700s, he spotted a problem we still haven't fixed: prima donnas are everywhere.

The truth is, it's not how you treat the CEO in the boardroom—it's how you treat the security guard in the lobby. The kind lady dishing out meatloaf in the cafeteria. The valet running around in the rain to grab your car. The crew that empties your trash after hours.

Be respectful, not dismissive. Acknowledge others and show a little humility. The world doesn't actually revolve around your presentation deck or portfolio website.

Find ways to put a smile on someone's face. Even a stranger.

[HUMILITY]

It's easy to be caught up in our own lives. Doing what works for us, even at the expense of others.

When you do right by others, life (and karma) have a way of coming around.

Kind. Respectful. Thoughtful.

If those are the words people bring to mind when your name comes up, you're doing more than making great ads, you're making the world a better place.

PRIZED PONIES

I'd just arrived at The Martin Agency, fresh from Los Angeles, riding in with a saddlebag of awards and the swagger of a prized pony.

In a few short months, our team's work for Mercedes-Benz was turning heads in the agency and I was asked to work on a new business pitch for a Boston company called PictureTel.

My partner and I did most of the heavy lifting on the creative, and the plan was for me to present the work in the meeting.

My moment. My stage. Cue the Rocky theme music.

But a few days before the pitch, the agency president came to me: "Would you mind if Kerry Feuerman—your boss—presented instead?"

With little hesitation, I assured him that I was comfortable, well-rehearsed and looking forward to presenting.

No thanks.

Why should I give up the spotlight? This was my chance to shine.

I put myself above the team and, surprisingly, they let me.

I was a good, confident presenter. I could get laughs. But

[HUMILITY]

Kerry was a different breed. He could flip a switch and light up the room.

I couldn't see it at the time. I was barely thirty years old, fueled by ego and my new position.

My presentation and the pitch went fine. The clients smiled at all the right places and were complimentary of the work.

But fine doesn't win the day. Kerry could've turned fine into fireworks. Instead, we walked away empty-handed.

We lost the pitch and I gained a valuable lesson.

Sometimes the right move isn't about proving yourself—it's about proving you're willing to put the team in the best position to win.

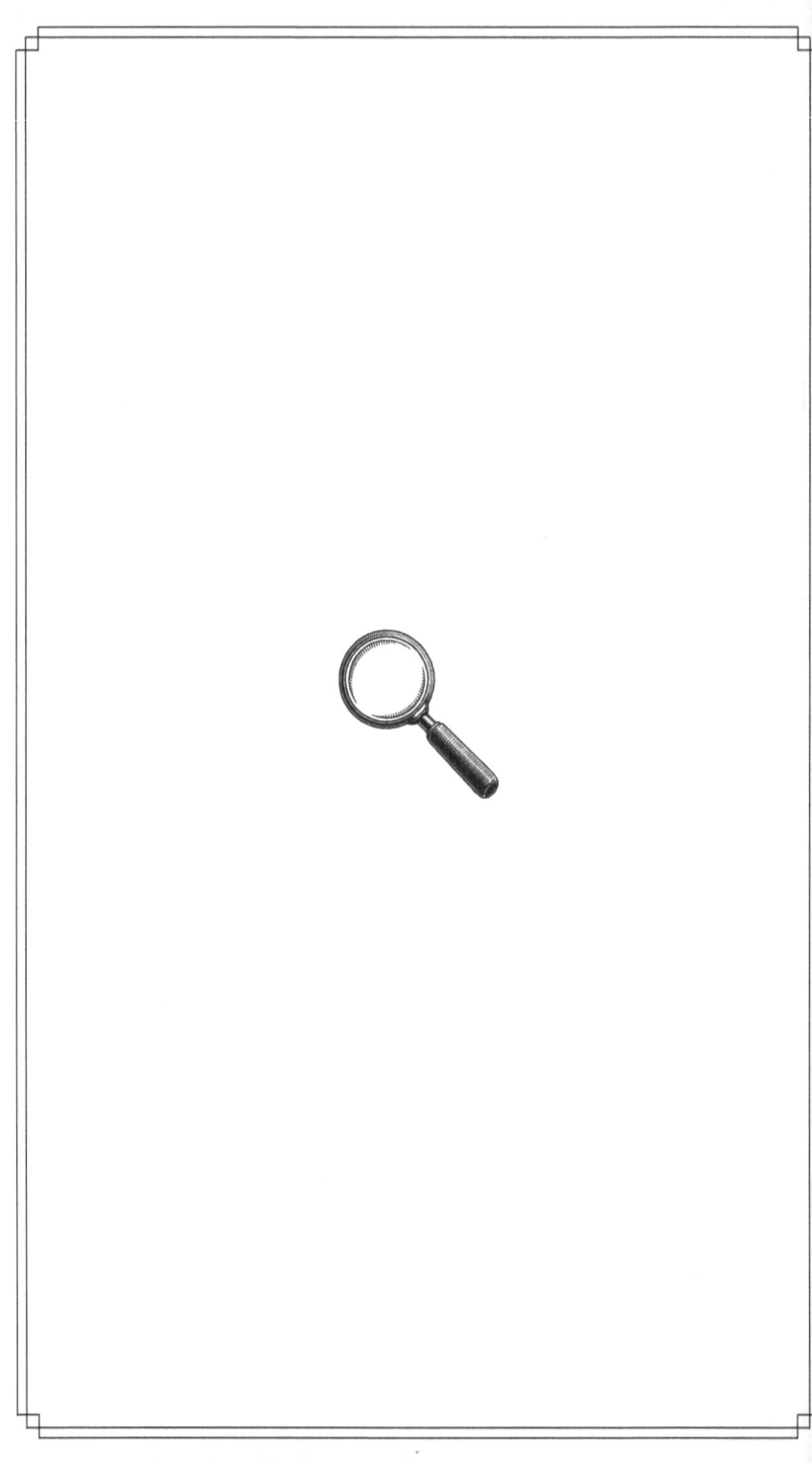

Step 6

PERSPECTIVE

Creative success often comes from looking beyond the obvious. Seeing what the others don't.

NO LAUGHING MATTER

———◆———

As creatives, we're expected to be funny. It's something we do well. But when my partner, Mark Fuller, and I received the Amgen creative brief, smiles faded, chuckles subsided and the sober reality set in.

Amgen makes a drug, Neupogen, which helps restore white blood cell counts in breast cancer patients. As we came to learn, many of these patients weren't knocking, but pounding on death's door.

Big gulp.

What could two creatives say that could, in any way, be comforting to someone in this situation? Even more challenging, we're two guys who have never faced anything amounting to breast cancer.

Empathy, honesty and optimism became our creative tools.

Our first ad depicted a woman, nude from her chin to her waist, covering her left breast with her right arm. It was a poignant image shot by *TIME* cover photographer, William Coupon. The headline: *You've just found out you have cancer, let's begin by reducing the lump in your throat.*

A second ad showed a young child placing her fingers to her mom's face. The mom wore a scarf on her head with the

[PERSPECTIVE]

headline: *The horrors of chemotherapy are true. They're also a decade old.*

Our ads hoped to instill a reason to believe. No miracle cure, but a mental helping hand.

The raw honesty of the campaign was recognized with an *MPA Stephen E. Kelly Award* as one of the Top 25 magazine campaigns of the year.

But in this case, any awards were byproducts of trying to do what was right for our client and their patients.

Without a doubt, it was my most difficult creative assignment and one of my most fulfilling.

EXPERIENCE ISN'T EVERYTHING

Clients often look for agencies deeply ingrained in their category. They want partners who speak the language, know the players and can recite the acronyms in their sleep.

But amazing creative work often comes from the outside looking in.

There's power in knowing just enough to be dangerous, but not so much to be jaded.

Fresh eyes, curiosity and imagination can lead you down creative paths the category insiders would never dream of taking.

At a recent conference, Neil Hoyne, Google's Chief Strategist, told a story that put category experience neatly in its place.

A pediatric trauma nurse applied for a job at Google. Her competition was tough: Two industry veterans with resumes that checked every box the position required.

On paper, she didn't stand a chance.

But her pitch caused the executives at Google to pause.

She explained how, every day in the trauma ward, she walks into the unknown. She never knows how many babies' lives will be hanging in the balance that day. Resources might

[PERSPECTIVE]

be stretched. Doctors might not be available. The unknown makes it hard to staff for. The situation changes minute by minute. And she's learned to make life-and-death decisions in that chaos.

She suggested to them that the best person for the job might be the one who knows the least about it.

She was hired two weeks later.

Talented, smart creatives can get up to speed on any product, any category, any client. Quickly. They know where to dig and what to look and listen for.

Creatively-driven agencies are full of talented problem solvers who don't see boundaries, just opportunities. They live to crack the code. Not repeat it.

The ability to skip beyond the tired, expected approaches is where smart clients can win.

WHAT IF IT WERE YOUR COMPANY?

It's easy to spend money when it's not coming out of your own pocket. As creatives, we're constantly pitching ideas to our clients and asking them to pay a handsome tab to produce them.

But recommending where and how clients spend their hard-earned marketing dollars isn't a casual endeavor.

Falling in love with our ideas is easy. Unexpected ideas. Funny ideas. Emotional ideas. The kind of ideas that create chatter and catch the attention of awards show judges.

Great ideas, yes. But are they the *right* ideas for our clients?

In prepping for a big creative presentation, our Account Director, Brad Armstrong, walked into my office. Campaigns were sprawled across the desk, the walls, the floors—a virtual creative smorgasbord of sorts.

Eager to share, we walked Brad through each idea. Carefully noting the strengths, weaknesses, the whole nine yards. While my mouth was running and my mind racing, he stopped me in mid-sentence with one simple question:

"What would you do if it were your company?"

Wait, my company? My money? My brand and reputation on the line? Suddenly, I wasn't just a creative trying to sell

[PERSPECTIVE]

an idea. I was thinking like a business owner considering an investment.

It completely changed my lens and my perspective.

When you're reviewing concepts, it's one of the best questions a creative person can ask themselves.

Would you push all your chips in on this idea? Would you stand in front of a boardroom of investors and passionately plead its case?

I'm not stumping for weaker, safer creative paths. They won't lead you to the promised land, only deeper into the forest of ubiquity.

Great work is simple. Thought-provoking. Unexpected. Unafraid.

When your ideas fire on all those cylinders—when it's work you'd stake your reputation on—that's when you know you're onto something.

ARGUING WITH MILLIONAIRES

Car dealers can be ruthless. Especially when they're judging creative work.

As I stood in front of a regional council of a dozen or so Philadelphia Mercedes-Benz dealers, sizing them up, it occurred to me: They were all considerably older and considerably richer than myself. Self-made millionaires. Their rounding errors could cover my paychecks.

Their business was selling cars, not buying funny ads. But I was armed, ready and just naive enough to be dangerous.

The new Mercedes C-Class had just rolled off the line with a starting price under $30,000. This was big news. The kind of news the dealers didn't want buried in the third line of body copy—even if it was bolded.

Luckily, I wasn't just presenting one ad, but a dealer tool kit full of ad executions.

To get what we wanted, which was smart, funny, potentially award-winning ads, I was going to start with giving them what they wanted: Something right to the point.

The first ad went up on the screen: a beauty shot of the new C-Class with the headline, *Did you know you can buy a Mercedes-Benz for under $30,000?*

[PERSPECTIVE]

Not exactly Cannes material. A creative flatliner, but simple, to the point and exactly what they were hoping to see.

Suddenly, the room relaxed. Smiles spread, heads nodded and arms uncrossed. I had managed to build a fragile bridge of trust with this group of seasoned skeptics.

That ad was my Trojan Horse. It kicked open the gate for smarter, more creative executions to follow.

I presented a range of funnier, more compelling ads. The dealers laughed, leaned in and listened.

They already had what they wanted.

Over a dozen of those little Mercedes ads found pages in *The One Show* that year.

You can't shove creativity down a client's throat. Give them a bite of what they want, then you have the freedom to serve up something a little tastier.

WHO'S ON FIRST?

In every agency, regardless of size, there are positions to play. Sure there are athletes out there capable of playing on both sides of the ball, but they're few and far between in advertising.

Focusing on your strengths, your role and where you fit on the team will not only make you better, but your agency better.

The trendy mantra these days is, "Everyone is creative!" I believe that's true. But channel that creativity in your respective role.

I want my media planner to be creative about how we reach people in new ways, where our ads show up, not what the headline should say.

I want my account executive unearthing meaningful consumer insights, not debating which take should make the cut.

Don't get me wrong. My oversized ears are open to ideas. But swim lanes, people.

When everyone starts trying to do everyone else's job, chaos and confusion take the field. Accountability goes out the window and a thick fog of indecision rolls in.

[PERSPECTIVE]

Great agencies, just like great teams, are stacked. They have all-stars at every position. What they don't have is a third baseman constantly asking to pitch because he logged a few innings in high school.

Sorry slugger, I have pitchers who've spent careers perfecting their breaking ball, I need you guarding the hot corner and snagging line drives.

Figure out what you do best, stake your position and work hard to do it better than anyone out there.

That kind of talent is always in demand.

FIRE THE CLIENT!

Clients can be difficult. Here's why: Most aren't genetically wired to spot, much less buy, truly great creative. Especially work that feels a bit outside their comfort zone.

That doesn't make them villains or idiots. It's their money, their brand, their prerogative.

When good work gets killed for bad reasons, it's more than frustrating. It's mind-numbing. Apocalyptic.

The kind of moment where you quietly slide all sharp objects out of reach.

Challenging clients don't just reject ideas. They drain you. Like vampires, they suck the creative juice right out of you. Leaving you pale, lifeless and possibly reconsidering a career in artisanal breadmaking.

It's tempting to yell, "Get rid of them!" Sometimes that is the smart move. Tough clients will wear you down, and worse, they'll rip and gnaw at the work until it's unrecognizable.

But firing a client isn't like ghosting a bad date. It comes with fallout.

Revenues take a hit. Sometimes that means staff cuts. Which makes "good riddance" feel a lot less good.

[PERSPECTIVE]

On the other hand, keeping a bad client can be a direct hit to the agency culture you're building.

Clients serve different needs and roles within the agency. Your largest client is usually not your best creative client. But they keep the lights on. They fund payroll. They give you the runway to do bold, career-defining creative work for those smaller, braver brands who get it and want it.

Every situation is unique. There is no right or wrong answer.

Protecting your agency culture is paramount. But before you make a client walk the plank, make sure you're ready to watch the treasure chest go overboard with them.

CIVIL WAR SOLDIERS

What would possess someone to stand around in a thick wool trenchcoat, musket at the ready, as the sweltering heat of a Georgia summer topped 90 degrees?

Some might call it a passion. Most call it crazy.

Still, every year, our Atlanta History Center client would hold their annual Civil War Experience, a Civil War reenactment with real characters in really hot, heavy uniforms.

One of the toughest challenges creatives face is trying to understand the audience you hope to reach. Put yourself in their boots, so to speak.

In this case, what would motivate someone to plunk down $20 to step 150 years back in time?

To complicate matters, we were faced with not one, but two, equally important target audiences who couldn't have been more different.

On one hand, we hoped to attract aging Civil War enthusiasts with a penchant for the smell of gunpowder and the stench of sweat-soaked wool.

On the other, suburban soccer moms armed with minivans, to-do lists and a bevy of kids who think heavily-bearded men speaking in a deep southern drawl is cool.

[PERSPECTIVE]

Creatively, we needed a silver bullet—even if it was a lead one.

We came up with an archival photo of a Civil War soldier in full uniform, standing expressionless, gazing warily at the camera.

On his back, we retouched a giddy toddler strapped into a baby backpack. The baby smiled ear to ear in stark contrast to the soldier's solemn stare.

The headline simply read: *A Civil War experience for the whole family.*

The results were all left on the field. Record turnout for the four-day event and creative accolades to boot.

EYES WIDE OPEN

For creatives, focus is a great thing. An essential thing.

But don't let it turn into blinders.

Whether we're concepting or executing, it's easy to get locked into one view, convinced it can only work one way: the way we have firmly cemented between our ears.

But many times in my career, I've actually stepped back far enough to see there was a better path. A smarter take, even with a few slight adjustments.

This actually happened to me while writing this book.

I was certain that it should be a daily reader. A creative devotional so to speak. Three hundred and sixty five nuggets of wisdom. One bite each day. Enough to feed a hungry creative soul.

I would not be swayed.

Then one night as I was drifting off to sleep, a new thought crept in. What if this wasn't a calendar of wisdom, but a roadmap you could follow, step by step, to reach creative paydirt?

Interesting.

[PERSPECTIVE]

My head raced with the possibilities making it hard to get much sleep.

The next morning, it not only made perfect sense. But it lit a fire in me to start reformatting, rewriting and reimagining.

Hopefully, I didn't screw it up.

Have passion for your ideas, absolutely. But learn to sleep on them with your eyes wide open.

STRANGE BEDFELLOWS

As humans, we're often drawn to people who are much like us. Similar sense of humor. Same taste in music. Same guilty-pleasure Netflix shows. It's comfortable. Familiar.

But as a creative director, I'm attracted to people whose minds turn a little differently than mine.

I love seeing a great concept and thinking, "Wow, I would *never* have come up with that. My brain doesn't even work like that."

All creatives are wired differently. That's a great thing.

When I'm hiring, I look for people who share my temperament and creative sensibilities. Creatives who believe in simplicity, recognize good ideas and know the difference between clever and cliché.

But I also look for creatives who might turn left when I choose right. People who might flip over the stones that I would blindly walk right past.

The best creative departments I've been a part of were all a patchwork of personalities: the carefree spirits seated alongside the stone-faced assassins—the kind of person who sits silent for an hour and then drops a dagger.

Creativity thrives on that mix.

[PERSPECTIVE]

I've written plenty about mentors and bosses, but I've learned so much from the creatives sitting right next to me.

How to handle rejection without sulking. How to celebrate wins without becoming unbearable. How to keep swinging even when your last ten ideas struck out.

Creativity is best in mixed company. Different brains firing on different wavelengths.

It takes all kinds to deliver exceptional thinking.

And there's nothing strange about that.

TAKE A HIKE

As you've discovered by now, coming up with ideas isn't like making biscuits.

You can't just roll the dough out, preheat the oven and wait 'til the ideas are golden brown.

There's no switch you can flip. No magic faucet you can turn.

Ideas aren't dispensed like bills from an ATM by simply entering your creativity PIN.

Staring at your computer screen or writing pad until greatness appears is a fruitless pursuit.

When I hit the creative wall, I unplug, lace up my shoes and get outside.

Nothing jumpstarts my brain like a long walk.

The crazy thing is, the minute you stop obsessing about solving the problem, your brain quietly gets to work.

Puzzle pieces click and dots begin connecting.

Science even backs it up. Walking floods your brain with endorphins—those little "feel-good" messengers that boost mood, reduce stress and loosen up the mental knots.

On walks I find ideas easily come to me. Sometimes out of

[PERSPECTIVE]

left field. I'm doing my brain and my body a favor.

So the next time you're grinding it out at your desk, hit the kill switch. Quit staring, quit stressing and go for a nice long walk.

The ideas will catch up.

PULL THE PLUG

Stop me if you've heard this one before.

The client presentation goes amazingly well. *"Lots of really smart thinking here, guys. Give us some time to digest and we'll get back to you."*

Days later, the account director walks into your office with the news: "They *love* the first direction, but we have some work to do."

At first, it may not seem too bad. Just a flesh wound. Maybe make the headline bigger, add a subhead or bold lead into the copy, and we're good to go.

But wait, there's more.

There is a chart we need to add. And someone mentioned the tone of the headline being a little cheeky. Can we lean a little more serious?

The copy, however, is great!

But we may need to bold or italicize a few words just for emphasis.

Ideas sometimes die slowly. Death by a thousand pinpricks.

It's no one's fault. But pushing a once great idea out into the

[PERSPECTIVE]

world after it's been hacked to unrecognizable bits doesn't do the client or the agency any good.

Build trust with your clients. Push back when you know the idea is being watered down. When the edges are being sanded too much. Protect the integrity and impact of the idea at every turn.

When an idea begins gasping for breath, show some empathy and act decisively.

The longer you keep it on life support, the harder it gets to pull the plug and start anew.

THE BLAME GAME

When things start to go sideways, and in this business things will, pointing fingers is a natural defense.

Creative briefs are promised, but come late. Strategies constantly morph and change.

Timelines are choked down from weeks to days.

Clients drag their feet on feedback.

Creative directors change their minds like the wind.

Trying to get a decent idea pushed to the finish line can feel like running a marathon in leg irons.

Whether you're a junior copywriter or an agency principal, take ownership of the situation. That doesn't mean taking the blame.

The smoldering mess you may find yourself immersed in may not be your fault, but it is your responsibility to steer out of the wreckage.

It's okay to be frustrated—you're only trying to do your job. It's healthy to fight for what's right. Create the opportunity to do good work and protect it at every turn.

But when all that fails, it's time to look for solutions.

[PERSPECTIVE]

The only way out of this is forward.

Choose to conquer, not complain and you'll build bridges, you'll gain the respect of those around you.

And respect is great currency in this business.

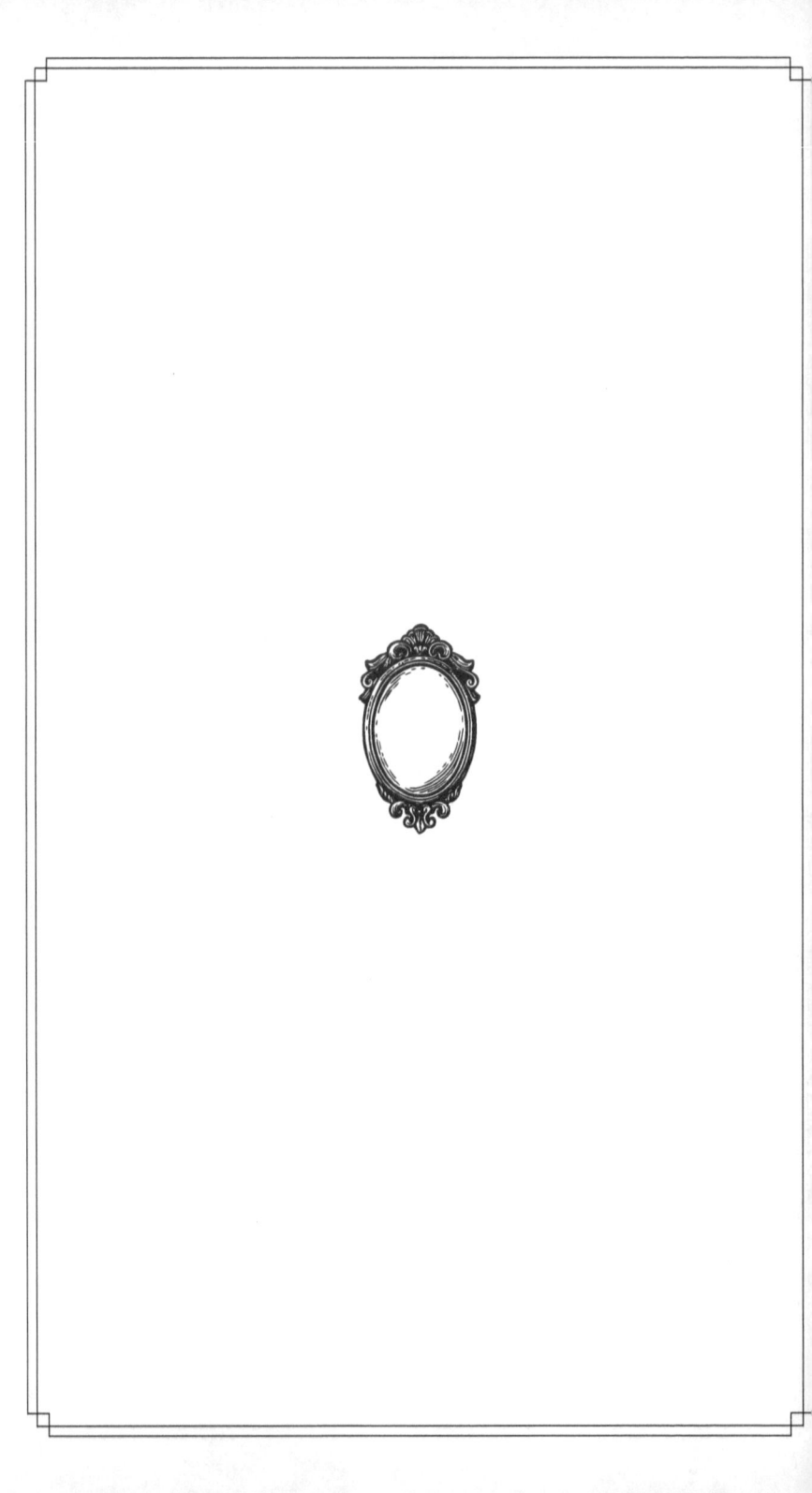

Step 7

HONESTY

There is no better policy in any profession. Honesty grows trust and respect. As a creative, that opens doors to great work.

THE DEVIL'S WATER

It's every creative team's dream: Your boss bursts into your office and announces, "We're pitching a new vodka account and I want you guys on it."

When our Creative Director, Tom Cordner, walked into my office and broke the news to my partner and me, our taste buds lit up.

Or at least mine did.

This wasn't some complicated software program that "improves logistics while optimizing real-time data analytics." This was friggin' vodka.

Simple. Sexy. Straight up.

As I leaned in for another sip of inspiration, my partner leaned back and quietly hung his head, he wasn't touching this one.

His faith had some pretty clear parameters and working on the devil's water didn't have a seat at the bar.

He calmly explained to Tom, "It's against my religious beliefs to work on an alcohol account."

Tom blinked. Then, without missing a beat, exploded: "JESUS. FUCKING. CHRIST!"

[HONESTY]

The irony still makes me laugh to this day.

Fortunately, we had a stable of art directors drooling to work on a vodka account and my partner was granted a pass.

Creatives come in all shapes, sizes and belief systems. That's part of what makes this business such a beautiful circus.

Stick to your principles. No campaign, no paycheck, no shiny statue is worth compromising what you believe in.

If your boss or agency has a problem with that, then you're at the wrong place.

There are far more important things in life than advertising—even vodka.

THE HALLWAY TEST

Few things make a creative person squirm faster than watching their precious ideas be judged—especially by someone who doesn't have 'creative' in their title.

It's understandable, but I'd suggest, misplaced.

Sharing your ideas isn't a threat, but an opportunity. The smartest ideas are easily spotted by everyone from account partners to interns to spouses—even the security guard manning the lobby desk.

Great ideas don't discriminate.

They don't care about income, religion, job description, or whether someone's rocking a necktie or a nose ring.

They just connect.

If your audience has to squint, connect too many dots, or hold a 'creative' badge to get it, odds are the idea isn't that great.

But here's the thing about sharing your work up and down the halls. You're looking for insights, not votes.

What's working or do we have a few loose wires? This isn't about approval ratings.

[HONESTY]

Second, this isn't a democracy. The creative director is the captain of this ship.

If that's you, your job is to take feedback, nod politely. Then implement where and if you see fit.

We're not asking for extra hands on the wheel.

Every creative director needs the authority and autonomy to say, "Thanks, this is all great input. Let us continue to polish the ideas. We'll let you know where we end up."

That's their job. To honestly and objectively listen and act accordingly.

The hallway test isn't where ideas go to die, but where they prove they can stand on their own.

CUTTING TIES

Hiring is easy, firing is hard. As a creative director, it's one of the first things you learn.

Climbing the creative ladder, you'll find some rungs are tougher to scale than others. Get ready to create less and manage more.

That's okay, it's just all part of a creative's evolution.

Building and steering a creative department is more than leading the work, that part is easy. It's also about managing the people and motivating the team.

At Huey/Paprocki, we had a young writer only a few years into his career. His talent was off the charts like a long distance runner with a hellacious kick.

He could give other writers a head start only to blow creatively by them when he decided to put pen to paper.

We were lucky to have this super-charged, eight-cylinder creative powerpack sitting right in our midst.

But our little agency needed him running at full speed. All pistons firing, pedal to the metal. All the time.

In reviews, we'd lay it out for him. He'd nod along in agreement. Then he'd push hard for a month or two,

[HONESTY]

delivering stellar work, but then take his foot off the gas.

The hard part about letting someone go is that you're firing more than an employee, you're firing a friend. This is especially true in smaller, tight-knit agencies.

What I knew in my heart though was that he'd land on his feet. He was too good. He'd built a great portfolio of work.

Soon, Chiat/Day in Los Angeles came calling. A few years later, he bounced to Cramer-Krasselt, working on Porsche. And later, BBDO on AT&T.

Needless to say, he's enjoyed a long, fruitful career.

At the time, letting him go was the right decision for us, but also the right decision for him.

I knew he was destined for great things and we remain good friends to this day.

WHO GIVES A SH*T?

A few years out of college, I packed up my portfolio and a healthy dose of courage and drove north from Atlanta to Richmond, Virginia.

I was hoping to share my creative work with any agency willing to listen.

At the time, I had no idea that I would be meeting with a long list of advertising dignitaries including Bill Westbrook, Mike Hughes, Kerry Feuerman, Luke Sullivan, Hal Tench, Jerry Torchia and others.

Bill had his own shop, Westbrook & Company, and generously gave this wide-eyed kid a half hour of his time.

We sat in a small conference room where a handful of rough concepts were pinned to the wall. Single sheets of paper, rough headlines scribbled in Sharpie, quick sketches beside them.

Bill stood there, arms crossed, scanning his work. Then, pointing to each concept, he turned to me and asked, with conviction: "Who gives a sh*t?"

I froze, unsure if I was supposed to have the answer.

That question was my first real lesson in how to judge creative work. If your idea doesn't matter—if it doesn't

[HONESTY]

connect, resonate or make anyone feel something—then it's just noise.

A waste of time and money.

That half hour with Bill reshaped how I would judge creative for the next four decades. I learned how to kill ideas quickly, mercifully, when they were meaningless.

I learned that rigor matters more than cleverness.

More than that, though, I realized that Bill wasn't just critiquing his own work. He was sharing his standards with someone who hadn't figured it out yet.

Someone looking for a creative compass.

These days, we call that paying it forward. Back then, it felt more like a masterclass in four simple words: Who gives a sh*t?

EVEN LAWYERS HAVE A FUNNY BONE

Clients often say, "We want to be edgy, have an attitude, disrupt the status quo." It sounds appealing, but most often, they don't really have an appetite for that type of work.

Sometimes, they do.

The Daily Report (a legal paper distributed to law firms across Georgia) had a new publisher, Steve Korn, at the helm and ready to stir the pot.

"Our paper is 130 years old," he told us. "We're stiff, stale, and we need to shake things up."

For us, this was an open invitation to put Steve's words to the test.

We presented five campaigns, one of which was so irreverent that we almost left it behind, but then decided, "Hey, it will at least be good for a laugh in the meeting."

One of the features of the newly revamped *The Daily Report* highlighted lawyers who had recently switched firms.

When we presented the first headline—*Read about where all your lawyer pals are going. Besides hell, of course.*—they virtually stood and applauded.

Even we were shocked.

[HONESTY]

Steve asked how quickly we could put that on a billboard facing the Regions Bank building, which was home to over a dozen law firms. Steve wanted to plant this little gem right under their eyeballs.

Other lines in the campaign included: *Writing that will inspire you. Possibly to sue someone.* As well as: *We follow lawyers closer than the private detectives hired by their wives.*

You'll hear me state many times that great creative work takes great clients. So here's to Steve Korn and his team at *The Daily Report*, for not just talking the talk, but laughing all the way through it.

SELLING WIDGETS

Why is most business-to-business advertising so damn boring?

We're still talking to people with a pulse and emotions just like any other human. These are not glassy-eyed robots who live only for the technical specs and product codes of the widgets they're looking to buy.

There's absolutely no reason B2B work can't feel like B2C. The same rules apply: keep it simple, make it engaging and memorable.

Maybe the problem is that a lot of B2B marketers think their products are too complex for creativity. Sure, selling cybersecurity software might sound trickier than selling beer or bubblegum. But that's why we have websites, brochures, and sales reps.

You don't have to explain everything in one ad.

Yet so many B2B clients can't resist. They want to toss six product benefits at you in hopes that you might catch one. What they don't realize is that people instinctively turn away from clutter and confusion.

The B2B landscape is overshadowed by a dark, murky cloud of mediocre advertising, but that's your opportunity.

[HONESTY]

You're not competing against Nike, BMW or Budweiser. Your competition is Reditech fasteners, Conrads Joist Supply and Built Better Ball Bearings.

If you can't outshine that competition, maybe it's time to surrender your laptop.

No matter what you're selling—whether it's industrial faceplates or something slightly more fascinating—treat your audience like they have a brain.

Make them think. Make them smile. Make them feel.

In the land of mechanized widgets, a little human touch goes a long way.

STOKING THE FIRE

Creatives are often fond of proclaiming, "If I had my own agency, I'd do things differently."

A statement usually born out of frustration, staring at a conference room table seeping with the fresh blood of slaughtered creative concepts.

A decade into my career, I decided to put that theory to the test. I was leaving Richmond in hopes of starting my own shop, which I did a year later with my partner, Joe Paprocki.

As I made the rounds at The Martin Agency, thanking everyone and unveiling my plans, I found myself standing at the door of Harry Jacobs.

Harry was a bear of a man who sat quietly at his neatly adorned desk. Calm, polite and razor-sharp, he was a legend in the business.

Harry was known to champion great work and chew up account executives like twice-eaten broccoli.

"Come in, Ron. Sit down," he offered, motioning me toward his desk.

"Harry," I began, "I want to thank you for everything and let you know that I'm moving to Atlanta to start my own shop."

[HONESTY]

He smiled. "Congratulations. What are you planning to do for new business?" He casually posed.

Confidently, I explained how I'd like three or four core clients and just focus on them. Not be distracted chasing new accounts.

Harry looked down and calmly shook his head. He sighed a sigh that only comes with wisdom earned the hard way.

"You have to constantly be looking for new business," he said. "Always."

It was advice that stuck.

From day one at Huey/Paprocki, we made prospecting a habit—reaching out to companies across categories, keeping a steady rhythm.

And it worked. Word spread. Referrals came. Phones started ringing.

So grab the poker. Add another log. Always keep the new business fires burning.

SOMEONE HAS TO SUFFER

Humor usually needs a loser. That's not cruel, it's the mechanics of a joke.

A guy bangs his head on an open file cabinet drawer and we all chuckle.

A bird bombs a shiny new car and we grin.

A runaway lawn mower chews through a freshly-planted flower bed. Cue the laughter.

Losers make us laugh and that's fine.

It's fine because it's not us. Look at that poor schmuck, glad it's not me.

To get a laugh, you often need a victim. And in the ad world, that makes some folks squeamish. Many want to soften the blow. Sand down the edges. Make it friendly and contact-free so no one gets hurt.

Humor loses its bite when you dull it down.

Ideas need edges. Sharp ones. Don't let your steak knives be reduced to butter knives.

Protecting ideas is your job. If someone in the room insists on neutering the joke, offer to pull the idea off the table.

[HONESTY]

Save it for another day, a braver client.

The willingness to walk away from an idea shows your belief in being true to the concept. In its best form. It reminds people where your creative bar is set.

Ironically, sometimes your ability to say no makes others decide to say yes.

So guard the punchline. Feed the absurdity. Let someone suffer—just a little—we all could use a good laugh.

HUMAN TRUTHS

Human truths hit people right between the eyes. They're unavoidable. They make people nod, laugh or groan because they've been there.

When your idea is rooted in a human truth, you have more than a puncher's chance of landing a blow squarely in someone's frontal lobe.

Human truths are everywhere. Babies cry on planes. Neighbors are nosy. Dark backroads are scary. Shopping carts are drawn to shiny metal doors.

Okay, there's four as fast as I can type. There are plenty, plenty more out there.

Ideas tied to a human truth are more relatable and more believable. It tells your audience, "We get you. We know what your life's like. We've been there, too."

Human truths are powerful because they connect emotionally.

Nike's "Just Do It" tagline and platform is a perfect example. It reminds us that even when we're tired, when it's raining, when our muscles are sore, we need to suck it up and get to it. Excuses are for those who finish second.

Dove's "Real Beauty" campaign is empowering because it's

[HONESTY]

honest, empathetic and bold enough to call B.S. on society's impossible beauty standards. It works because it's eye-opening and real.

Snickers famously stated, "You're Not You When You're Hungry." There's a human truth. Who hasn't been hangry? The campaign used everyday people who transformed into celebrity personas because they're hungry.

Ideas based in human truths are almost always simple. They cut straight through and connect with something deep, universal and undeniable. They cross cultures and societies.

So every time I sit down to concept, that's where I start: Find the truth. Then build an idea around it.

The closer you can get to what's real, the closer you get to what works.

TAKE IT PERSONALLY

I once had a creative director tell me that they took every new business loss personally.

At first, I didn't get it.

But he knew better than anyone that advertising isn't just an idea business—it's a people business.

Clients aren't just buying the work, they're buying you.

It's a lot like dating and when you're kicked to the curb for the cuter, smarter agency, it stings.

The secret to winning is access early and often. You need to start building that relationship before you're sitting in some meat-locker of a conference room, nervously clicking through a deck.

Presenting to a room of strangers is an uphill climb with loose impediments and long falls. It's easy to do a faceplant. It's far better to present to someone you know. Or even kinda-sorta know.

Early meetings with a prospective client can tell you a lot.

Are they open-minded? Are they looking for creative work that will set their brand apart? Are they nice, respectful humans?

[HONESTY]

First impressions rarely lie.

Choosing which clients to chase after can be tricky. No agency likes to lose. But the only way to be turned down by a client is to first agree to participate in a pitch.

Remember: It's not mandatory.

I always use early capabilities meetings to decide if this is a piece of business and a client that's a good fit for us.

If it's not someone you'd like to break bread with, it's not worth breaking out a scope of work.

Don't chase anything and everything. Don't be blinded by dollar signs. Fattening your bottom line for the wrong account can poison your culture.

And in this business, culture is everything.

Remember: With every new opportunity, you're sizing them up as much as they're scrutinizing you.

NITWITS

Some brands love to toss around bold claims like confetti. We're the best! We're #1! We're the leader!

As if everyone will just nod along and buy it. They won't.

A client once asked me, "Why do we need to be creative? Can't we just say we're the best?"

First off, declaring greatness doesn't make it true. More likely, it makes people suspicious.

My response to the client was, "Well, if we are the best, then we need to prove it."

We live in a show me, not tell me culture. What sets your brand apart? More durable? Better tasting? Kick-ass customer service?

Deeming you're the best is something the customer has to arrive at.

Bill Bernbach, the creative Godfather of Doyle Dane Bernbach, figured this out long before most of us were born.

In the 1960s, he built an agency on the then-radical notion that consumers should be treated like actual thinking humans, not nitwits to be duped with loud claims and shiny promises.

[HONESTY]

Bill famously proclaimed, "The truth isn't the truth until people believe you, and they can't believe you if they don't know what you're saying. They can't know what you're saying if they don't listen to you, and they won't listen to you if you're not interesting. You won't be interesting unless you say things imaginatively, originally and freshly."

That's still the gospel.

To earn attention and trust, you have to be interesting, unexpected and, yes, entertaining. You have to make people want to listen.

That's something that even nitwits will sign up for.

FIRST BLUSHES

Great work is instantly recognizable.

It elicits quick reactions. Smiles spread and eyes light up. You don't give it a second thought because you don't have to.

Unfortunately, advertising is filled with doubters, skeptics and overthinkers.

Everywhere you turn, people are poking, prodding and overanalyzing.

When I'm presenting concepts, I'm on full radar mode, scanning the room for facial reactions.

Very few clients have a good poker face. When an idea genuinely strikes, it's hard to hold back.

Usually, you know in the first few seconds if an idea is a winner.

So why do so many great ideas die on the chopping block?

Because as soon as the gut reaction passes, the mind barges in. It begins to pick things apart. It looks for foundational cracks in thinking, chinks in the armor.

It begins to slice and dice the idea until there's only table scraps remaining.

[HONESTY]

In this mighty struggle, the left brain starts kicking the right brain to the curb.

Instead of focusing on what's right about the idea, we look for reasons it's not working. Or worse yet, start imagining them.

Second-guessing our first reactions.

But the best clients stick to their gut. They trust their instincts. They're bold and brave, but not reckless.

They know a big idea is bound to stop people in their tracks, turn heads. Even create a few butterflies.

And they feel it at first blush.

WESTERN WEAR

Montana is famous for its sweeping vistas and stunning skies. It's a canvas painted with weathered faces, calloused hands and well-worn denim.

You won't find a three-button polo anywhere in sight.

By week three of a Wrangler Jeans shoot, I was getting pretty comfortable in cowboy country. Spending your days and nights around cattle, cowhands and the smell of dust and leather, makes you want to throw on a Stetson hat and try your luck at roping a bull. (Don't do it.)

I decided to mosey into town and bought a couple of authentic Western shirts. Dual chest pockets. Pearl snaps. Sharp.

Butch Cassidy and the Sundance Kid would have given me a thumbs-up.

I definitely looked the part, but I didn't feel it.

Once I boarded the plane back East, I felt even more out of place. I wasn't a cowboy, I was a poser.

I was pretending to be something I wasn't.

For months, I could never get comfortable in my new Western shirts and they were exiled to the far corner of my closet.

[HONESTY]

Waiting for the next trip to Goodwill.

As creatives, we're tempted to dress clients in creative clothes and campaigns that are fun for us, but not at all right for them.

Establishing an authentic brand voice and visual aesthetic is everything. It shouldn't tie your hands creatively, but free your thinking. It gives you a clear, defendable bullseye to aim for.

I've been guilty of serving up ideas that didn't quite fit—like a plaid sport coat that was just a size too small—hoping my client might somehow squeeze in.

Even when I've sold those ideas through, I've regretted it later. The clients were never fully bought in and, worse yet, it undermined the trust that I'd worked so hard to build.

Brand voice matters. Get it right, don't sway.

And unless you're from west of the Mississippi, don't ever show up in a Western shirt with dual chest pockets and pearl snaps.

Step 8

INITIATIVE

Success won't find you.
Be ready to explore new frontiers
without fear of the unknown.

MAKE YOUR OWN START

I was a wide-eyed boy from a small town who somehow managed to stumble off the University of Georgia campus and straight through the doors of J. Walter Thompson's Atlanta office.

At the time, JWT was the largest ad agency in the world.

I wasn't a prized draft pick or hotshot recruit that was wooed over from a crosstown agency. No, far from it.

I was an intern on a short three-month leash with no promise of a full-time paycheck.

Still, I was in.

From day one, my mission was to find a way to stick in an industry that often feels Teflon-coated.

At the time, JWT was running an ad campaign touting their star clients. The campaign used headlines such as *J. Walter Thunder* for the Ford Thunderbird and *J. Walter Thrill* for Six Flags amusement parks.

It was a smart campaign with an ownable twist.

I figured: If an agency could run ads touting their clients, why not one touting their people?

[INITIATIVE]

Under the cover of darkness, working with a friend in the art studio, I cobbled together an ad with this headline: *J. Walter Investment.* It sat above a photo of a twenty-three-year-old me grinding away at my desk like I belonged there.

The copy I wrote explained how investing in young talent would boost the agency's future success.

Late one Thursday night, I printed a few copies and placed them on the three senior executives' desks.

By 9 a.m. Friday morning, I wasn't an intern anymore.

Nothing in this business is handed to you. You have to create your own opportunities.

And sometimes, your own ads.

WHY WAIT?

Creatives famously whine about needing more time to concept.

They're not wrong.

Our brains aren't vending machines. You can't just pull a lever and expect a bag of hot, crunchy ideas to tumble out like toasted cheese crackers.

We are often, however, our own worst enemies.

We wait for someone to schedule an internal meeting.

We stall until someone can get a client call lined up.

We drag our heels until someone finds time to write a brief.

Yes, clear input and direction matter, but the more we wait, the more we sabotage ourselves.

Unfortunately, deadlines rarely move.

If you know an assignment is coming, start stirring the pot early. Be in your account person's or brand planner's ear.

Push the timeline forward so you have time to breathe on the back end. Time is our only window to generate ideas, then have time to reflect and improve them.

[INITIATIVE]

Get your conceptual wheels turning even before the brief touches down. I've found that, at times, I'll go down the wrong rabbit hole, but beginning to peel back the onion—even without specific direction—is still time well spent.

Don't let agency and client inefficiency screw you. Because it will. No one will care or remember that you didn't have enough time to concept.

Except you.

And excuses never play well on the back end.

Protect your process. Guard your time like gold. That's the only way you're going to deliver what everyone wants: Not just ideas, but great ideas.

COMPLACENCY KILLS

Cal Ripken, a Hall of Fame shortstop and holder of baseball's record for most consecutive games played at 2,632, logged 20 seasons.

Each of them with one club, the Baltimore Orioles.

Cal's lucky he wasn't in advertising.

Moving up in this business likely means moving around. Wearing a few different uniforms.

It's easy to get comfortable, but if you want to jump from charter buses to private jets, stay open-minded.

It may be at a crosstown agency you've always admired. Or a call from a headhunter across the country.

When opportunity knocks, take a look out the peephole.

It may be a chance to jump client-side. Over the last decade, a surge of brands have built out their internal capabilities to either complement, or replace, agency partners.

Some are doing it well. Andy Pearson at Liquid Death, Paul Keister at Carvana and Brian Brooker's work at Garmin.

A new position can also mean new responsibilities, including managing creative teams.

[INITIATIVE]

As a right-brained person, I get that trading in your sketch book for a spreadsheet makes you want to spit up a little in your mouth.

We all got into this business to create—not to jump from meeting to meeting, supervise timesheets, or babysit a bunch of whiny creatives.

But if you don't move up in this business, you're usually moved out.

Consider your opportunities carefully. Make them at the right times for the right reasons. This isn't a race to the finish, rather a smart, steady uphill climb.

PUT YOUR BEST EAR FORWARD

We are in the business of persuasion, which usually requires using our words.

But it's quite possible that our greatest weapon is our ears.

Talking about ourselves comes easy. The amazing work we've done. The clients we've helped succeed. The awards crowding our lobby shelves.

But no one likes someone who can't shut up. Can't take a breath. Whether it's a coffee shop or a conference room, diarrhea of the mouth is never a good look.

Understandably, talking about ourselves is a difficult habit to break. We want to put our best foot forward—even if it's tongue first.

We want to tell prospective clients why we're the perfect fit. Why our strategic process and creative work will lead them to Camelot.

Pump the brakes. Don't be so eager.

Agencies who have mastered the art of listening, are usually stacking wins.

When you listen, it shows confidence and maturity.

[INITIATIVE]

There's no sense of panic or urgency.

No need to 'close the deal.'

No fear that the big fish might shake the hook from its mouth.

Hearing what keeps a client up at night puts them in the spotlight, not you. When you can get to the bottom of what they really need, you can start offering real help.

Great work is only great if it works for our clients.

The more you ask, the more you know and the better your chance of delivering big, compelling ideas.

SHOW BUSINESS

As creatives, we love to think of ourselves as artists. Tortured. Brilliant. Slightly misunderstood.

But if you're in the business of selling creative concepts, you're also in show business.

You better be prepared, entertaining, ready for anything your audience throws your way.

In his book, *The Five Deadly Sins of Presenting Creative Work*, former Global Creative Director, Kerry Feuerman, explains how coming up with great work isn't enough.

The true test: Can you sell it?

Early on, I assumed great creative work would sell itself.

It doesn't.

Just like a great joke, great work needs the proper setup. You've worked hard on your material, don't let it die on the stage.

Don't assume it will all fall neatly into place.

Always start with the strategy, that's where your client starts. What are the insights and inspiration that led you down this creative path?

[INITIATIVE]

Remind everyone why being fresh, different and brave actually matters.

When tough questions come, don't panic or get defensive. Don't try to solve it on the spot. Take a breath and thoughtfully offer, "Great question, let us get back to you on that."

Calm confidence beats defensiveness every time.

In the early days of Fallon McElligott, when account executives met with clients, they were told: "If you don't sell the creative work, don't bother coming back."

In hindsight, this seems unfair.

The account folks didn't come up with the ideas. They can't discuss the process, the ideas discarded along the way, or the brilliant detours.

No one can sell the work like the people who created it.

The best agencies know that. They put creatives front and center when it's showtime.

So if you're one of those creatives, you better learn how to own the stage.

Don't be afraid to fail. You've put the work in. Now tell the world why it's great.

WEST COAST SHUFFLE

If your career is going to take off, you're going to need a few breaks. Mine came when the phone rang with a 310 area code.

A headhunter from Los Angeles had seen a NAPA Auto Parts TV campaign in the *Communication Arts Advertising Annual*. One that my partner, John Boone, and I had produced.

I was a mid-level copywriter in Atlanta working on glamorous accounts like Flav-O-Rich dairy products and Weyerhaeuser wood siding.

Los Angeles seemed like a long way away. But with one cat and zero reason to stay in Atlanta, my ears were wide open.

The Shalek Agency, a hot, up-and-coming shop in Santa Monica, needed a writer. They had recently won a slew of awards for the game show the $100,000 Pyramid as well as a very cool campaign for a surfing apparel brand, GOTCHA.

I flew out, interviewed, and a week later, I was a 28-year-old copywriter with a new job and a one-way ticket to the City of Angels.

What I didn't know was that my direct flight was about to hit turbulence.

Upon landing at LAX, my new art director partner picked me up and casually announced that she was taking a job with

[INITIATIVE]

Ogilvy in Hong Kong.

What?

I was due to start at Shalek the coming week when my headhunter called. "Ron, how would you like to join your old art director partner at Team One working on the Lexus account?"

Another plot twist.

I started at Shalek on Monday and interviewed at Team One on Tuesday. This was crazy.

On Thursday, I got the offer from Team One. With my stomach churning and head spinning, I walked into Shalek on Friday and resigned, less than a week into the job.

I started at Team One the following Monday.

I'm not one to break commitments, but this one felt life-altering. And it was.

Sometimes in your career, unforeseen opportunities arise. Flight plans change. If it seems like the right move, don't be afraid to change your itinerary.

A 246-MILE PUSH

What lengths will you go to to win a piece of business?

At Huey/Paprocki, we were young, hungry and up for pretty much anything.

We landed in a new business pitch for Bloom, a regional grocery store chain based in Charlotte, North Carolina.

To show how badly we wanted their business, we pushed a Bloom shopping cart from their store in Charlotte to our office in Atlanta.

Okay, we didn't push it the entire 246 miles, but we came damn close, filming every step of the way.

Our stunt started in a Bloom store with Danielle Bryson, our Account Executive, posing as a busy, on-the-go shopping mom. She perused the aisles, loading her basket, and then, upon checkout, headed out the door to the parking lot.

Only, instead of stopping at her car, she pushed her cart through the parking lot, toward the on ramp for I-85 south to Atlanta.

We stopped filming, threw the cart (and Danielle) in the back of our Art Director Aaron Thornton's Toyota 4-Runner and jumped on the highway.

[INITIATIVE]

Along our four-and-a-half hour trek, we filmed Danielle pushing her cart past apple stands, water towers and other landmarks along the way.

Sun beating down, sweat beading up. Yes, Danielle was a trooper.

The final scenes showed Danielle pushing the cart across the Jackson Street bridge with the Atlanta skyline as a backdrop, then through the doors of our agency.

The video ended with an art card reading: Hire an agency that's willing to go the distance.

It was an awesome stunt.

If you're wondering if we won the business, we didn't.

The client kindly asked where her shopping cart was. It was in our storage closet and soon returned to its rightful owner.

Sometimes you go out on a limb and it breaks beneath you. There's no shame in that. Just dust yourself off and keep climbing.

BISCUITS AND ROLLERCOASTERS

Two years into my advertising career, I had an epiphany.

I was a creative trapped in a young account executive's body.

Somewhere between the University of Georgia and J. Walter Thompson, I'd clearly taken a wrong turn. Likely at the intersection of 'Follow your passion' and 'Take the first job you can find.'

Part of my job, as a junior account executive on the Six Flags Amusement Park account, was to run interference between our creative department and our client.

I was the messenger, a human shield, wedged between client feedback and a hallway of creative malcontents.

You know, the place where bullets fly.

Fortunately, my good friend, Ken Lewis, was the copywriter on the account. Ken was incredibly smart but about as friendly as a honey badger on a three-day hunger strike.

Ken welcomed client suggestions like a root canal. Any suggestions. On this particular day, there were many.

The assignment was a radio spot, a promotion between Six Flags and Hardee's fast food restaurants. The script had already been sliced, diced, battered and put through the frier.

[INITIATIVE]

And in Ken's mind, mentally tossed into the green dumpster out back.

I knew even more copy changes would not sit well with Ken, but I had a plan.

I walked into his office and offered to make the copy changes myself. No one had to know. He could wash his hands of it. Before I could finish my offer, Ken eagerly accepted.

"Sure, Ron, now get out of my office."

It was a bold move, but if I had any chance of changing my job title to 'creative,' I needed to start building a portfolio.

That forgettable radio spot, some spec print ads and an outdoor board or two were enough to help me scale the wall out of account service and into a copywriting job.

You gotta start somewhere.

PICK UP THE PHONE

Sometimes hearing your voice means far more than reading your words.

A call is not only more personal, it can't be misread or misconstrued.

These days, we often hide behind emails, texts, chats and DMs like digital ninjas. They've become shorthand for "I'm too busy to talk to you right now."

They're an easy crutch to lean on. Quick. Convenient. They definitely make our work lives more efficient. And anyone who knows me knows that I champion efficiency.

There are times when a quick text to say, "Got it" or "Running late" is the right move.

Other times, a perfectly crafted email allows you to say exactly what you want to say, exactly how you want to say it.

But sometimes you need to go old school.

Pick. Up. The. Phone.

Even if you need to leave a voicemail, a little bit of effort can put a smile on someone's face.

Phone calls provide a human touch and can deliver a tone

[INITIATIVE]

and emotion that is being increasingly short-circuited in this digital age.

And here's a bit of irony: Sometimes phone calls actually save time. Things can be sorted out in seconds, instead of ping-ponging back and forth for hours on emails.

Phone calls build trust, rapport and relationships.

So do yourself a favor, find a moment to just pick up the phone to say, "Hi."

It's quick, easy, and reminds people that there's a living, breathing human behind every message.

The inbox can wait.

WHO'S THE BOSS?

Creative directors, even the good ones, need to kill things. It reminds them, and everyone else, who's in charge.

At Team One, we had a great Creative Director in Tom Cordner. Tom was a bright mind with the temperament of an overly-caffeinated Jack Russell terrier.

He recognized smart thinking when he saw it and surrounded himself with a hallway of talented creatives. That's what the best coaches and managers do.

But even the best leaders have blind spots.

Tom's would flare up after extended time away from the office.

We learned early on to never present concepts on Tom's first day back from vacation or a long TV shoot.

That was creative suicide.

From Tom's perspective, everything suddenly looked tired. Nothing was fresh enough or smart enough. And Tom would let you know that.

Yep, the sheriff's back in town.

Once back in the office, creative teams would rush to get on

[INITIATIVE]

Tom's crowded dance card. Teams lined up in the hallway, eager to show their ideas.

But my partner and I knew the trap. We sat back and waited.

Like lambs led unknowingly to slaughter, we'd watch teams file out of Tom's office, heads down, frustration setting in.

We knew that once Tom had reasserted his place in the pecking order, it was safe to slide in.

Most often, it worked like a charm.

It was a good lesson early in my career: Know your audience. Learn the temperament, quirks and blind spots of whomever you're presenting to—bosses and clients included.

Knowing what you're walking into is your best defense against unexpected casualties.

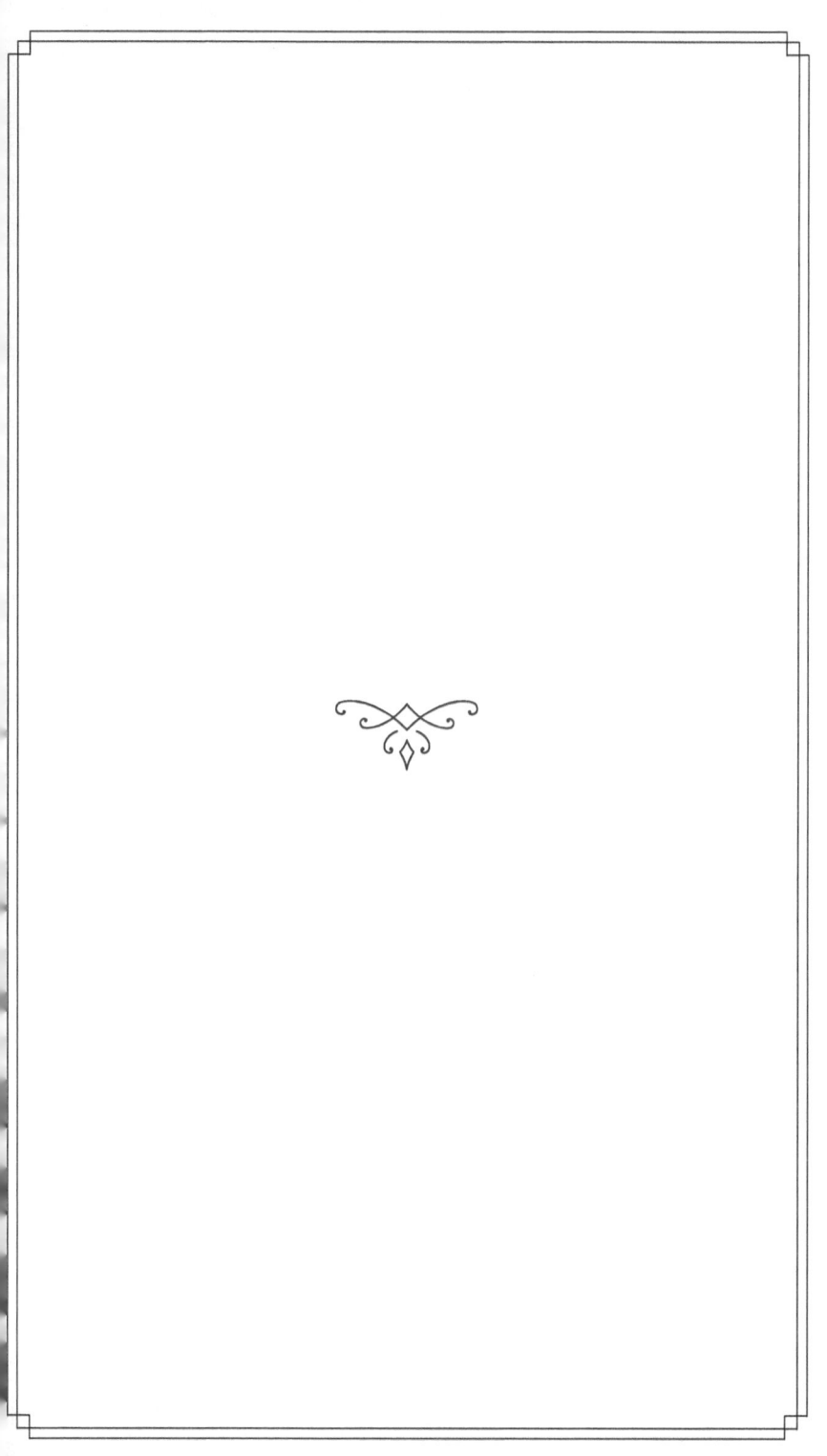

Step 9

DISCIPLINE

Your career path will take many twists and turns. Buckle up and keep your eyes on the road ahead.

IT'S ABOUT TIME

Creatives are notorious for being fashionably late.

Late for work. Late for internal meetings. Late for the agency 'koombayas' designed to create bonding experiences across all departments.

Who would be late for that?

We might want to say, "Better late than never." But in truth, it's not a good look.

Being late says, "I don't care that much. I've got better things to do. My time is more important than yours."

You earn the respect of those around you when you are prompt and prepared.

Not a prima donna.

Be on time and when time is up, say, "Thanks, but I've got work I need to get to." No need to linger.

Creatives need time to get the work done. Protect your time, it's your most precious resource.

Yes, it would be nice to skip out of meetings and possibly fall mysteriously ill on those agency fun days. But if you're part of a team, your presence matters.

[DISCIPLINE]

Your daily calendar can be your most useful weapon. Block out concepting time just like it were a meeting. It is, after all, a meeting of the minds. Schedule your day with the precision of a Swiss watch.

Whether you're in the office or not, people will constantly be vying for your time and attention. Some meetings matter. Some do not.

If you haven't noticed yet, some people like to meet just to meet.

Don't be sucked into the meeting vortex.

Creatives don't just throw ideas at walls. They need time to craft, tweak and polish them until they stick.

If you need to say "no" to a meeting, do it.

And when you absolutely have to be there, show up on time and once the meeting wraps, promptly exit.

There's work to be done and time is ticking.

KILL YOUR DARLINGS

Editing your ideas is a ruthless occupation. Some must die for others to live.

Whether it's your personal portfolio or your agency's website, deciding what stays and what gets tossed into the creative dumpster, is never easy.

Often, the temptation is to include a little bit of everything—a creative smorgasbord of sorts—because everyone has different tastes, right?

True. But this isn't Golden Corral.

You need to edit vigorously. Only your best work deserves the spotlight.

Mediocre ideas drag down the brilliant ones. They make creative directors second-guess your judgment. They make headhunters scratch their noggins in wonder. And they make pitch consultants question whether your agency can tell good from just kinda okay.

For me, a solid entry-level portfolio should have four or five comprehensive campaigns that prove your ideas can stretch across all platforms.

Sprinkle in a few one-offs. I love one-offs. Whether it's a killer outdoor board, an interactive idea, a stunt, even a bumper

[DISCIPLINE]

sticker. These are just small ideas that pack a big punch.

One-offs are like lightning bolts that your audience didn't see coming.

As you rise through the ranks, your portfolio will naturally grow. Post only your best work. You don't need a herd, only your show horses.

When I interviewed for my first creative director job, I had a decade's worth of ad campaigns under my belt. But I only put 15 pieces in my portfolio. Each one had found its way into an awards show index somewhere. No clunkers, no excuses, no second-guessing.

As a creative, you have to be willing to 'kill your darlings.' Edit your portfolio like a heartless hitman, even if it means discarding pieces you personally love.

Regardless of your audience, serve up only the cream.

TOO MANY COOKS

It's hard for any creative to work in a vacuum. Solving it yourself rarely happens. So it's natural to put our heads together.

But be wary of too many heads, too many hands, and too many opinions.

Ideas need crafting, not crowdsourcing.

The trend in many agencies is to cram everyone in a room, toss ideas around, and see what sticks.

On some level, I get it. We're all smart people with varying backgrounds and interesting thoughts.

But somewhere between the loud chatter, the laughter and the inevitable question—"Is lunch being brought in?"—you realize no one's steering the ship here.

The art and science of creativity has been reduced to a game of pin the tail on the donkey. Spitting out ideas with little thought or scrutiny.

There is no accountability in this scenario, my friends. Just noise.

Coming up with ideas is all fun and games until someone has to do the hard work of connecting the dots. Making sure the

[DISCIPLINE]

ideas are fresh, relevant and memorable.

As creatives, we're trained to mentally check these boxes in real time while discarding ideas that don't meet the criteria.

Advertising doesn't need more Swiss Army knives, it needs specialists.

If you're new to the agency world, come in with a clear focus, know your strengths, and have an idea of exactly where you want to fit.

Find what you do best, then do it better than anyone else out there.

Leave the brainstorming to more trivial tasks like naming the conference rooms.

SLOPPINESS

When I met my future wife, Judy Moran, she was a rising media maven at Team One in Los Angeles. My creative partner and I had just joined the agency, and with the creative department bursting at the seams, our makeshift office became the media conference room.

Not the worst fate as we were working amidst a gaggle of twenty-something-year-old media girls with bright minds and well-earned tan lines.

Each morning, I'd pass Judy and the others in the hall on my way to our "office." It didn't take long to learn that Judy was a stickler for details. A perfect trait for a media planner.

No one likes when the numbers don't add up.

Judy had zero tolerance for sloppiness and errors. If she received a resume or cover letter with a typo, it was tossed like 3-day-old coffee grounds.

Knowing Judy was hiring for an entry-level position, I simply couldn't resist.

I put my copywriting skills to use and submitted an application neatly addressed to Ms. Judith Moron.

It went something like this:

[DISCIPLINE]

Dear Ms. Moron,

I'm a big fan of yours and can't imagine a better mentor than you, Ms. Moron. I know I can be a valuable addition to your team, Ms. Moron…

You get the idea.

Judy didn't marry me for my intelligence, but my sense of humor may have sealed the deal.

Sloppiness, however, is no joke. It's a slick floor waiting to drop you to your knees.

There's no excuse for it. Copywriters should scrub every character. Art directors, every pixel.

Whatever your role, make sure that everything that leaves your desk reflects your best work—and your agency's.

There's no place in our business for sloppiness.

Or for morons.

HOOKS AND JABS

Great boxers don't spring from their corner throwing wild haymakers. They stalk. They study. They wait.

Left jab. Left jab. Left jab. And when the moment presents itself, right hook—BOOM!

The best advertising works the same way. It catches you off guard.

Great ads sneak up on you, they draw you in, then smack you squarely on your frontal lobe.

As creatives, we tend to obsess over the hooks, the knockout punches. But the jabs are essential, they're the set-up needed for the hook to find its mark.

For me, concepting always starts with jabs. Small, simple thoughts. Quick hits.

Getting as many ideas out as possible. Searching for the small, believable nuggets that can grow into bigger, more unexpected swings.

Get your thoughts down in plain English, straightforward and easy to understand. There will be time later to be more creative. Avoid trying to be too clever and asking your audience to work too hard.

[DISCIPLINE]

Start by making sense.

But let's not stop there. Now you can start exploring more nuanced ways to make the same point. More interesting routes that lead to the same place.

Tease your audience, intrigue them, invite them in.

Many brands want to skip right to the punchline. Avoid the courtship. It's understandable. Why not just tell your customers what you want them to hear?

But force-fed product messages usually fall on deaf ears. There's no joy in bludgeoning someone with benefits and surely, no reward for the consumer.

Lure your audience in, then hit them with something they never saw coming.

SCOPE CREEP

In advertising, the work you agree to and the work you actually end up doing are often two very different things.

New requests come in. Priorities shift. The 'scope of work' that seemed perfectly spelled out in the proposal begins to stretch, bend and rip like a chew toy caught between two pit bulls.

Whether you're a freelancer flying solo or part of a 300-person agency, clients will—intentionally or not—start to stretch the boundaries. Move the goal posts.

Often it's not their fault, it's just that suddenly they need things they didn't know they needed when they signed on the dotted line.

It's all okay, but you need to protect yourself.

Set clear boundaries and reinforce them often. Be honest. Be fair. Let clients know where they stand at all times.

Clients appreciate transparency. They don't like being blindsided.

Get it all in writing. It doesn't have to be complicated. Just a simple document outlining the deliverables, timing and fees. That document becomes your safety net when the additional requests start to fly.

[DISCIPLINE]

Send weekly status reports. Track your hours. Stay on top of the details. When you let things slip, you invite confusion and questions you might not want to answer.

Retainers and project fees are the fuel that keep the agency engine running.

Get invoices out early, keep your tank full, and remember, the work you serve up is not a bottomless cup.

DOLLARS AND SENSE

When we started Huey/Paprocki, we were all about the work. But we were also all about keeping the lights on.

Creativity and finances don't always make the best suitemates.

We stayed purposely lean. Our desks and chairs weren't from Herman Miller, but instead, Miller's Salvage Yard.

In the back room, we built shelving units out of discarded two-by-fours and plywood. Think less *Architectural Digest* and more *DIY Warehouse* chic.

It wasn't about being cheap, but smart.

Staying fiscally responsible gave us the freedom to choose the right clients, work on our terms, and let the work—not the lobby chandelier—do the talking.

One thing was for sure, when clients hired us, at least we knew it wasn't for our decorating tastes.

Running lean helps you weather the storms when they hit. And they will.

Clients leave. Landlords raise the rent. Teams need well-deserved raises.

[DISCIPLINE]

Most important, when you know your finances are in order, you can lay plans for the future. You're safeguarded when the unexpected hits.

Our intent was always to build our agency brick by brick, dollar by dollar, person by person.

All we needed was whatever was needed to do the work. We weren't interested in trying to look the part, we were selling the work hanging on the walls.

Few things will steal your sleep like shaky finances.

Don't let it.

Get the balance sheet rock solid, and your brain is free to chase the work.

MONSTER MASH

Frankenstein isn't going to win any beauty contests.

That's something we can all agree on.

So why are clients sometimes tempted to mash ideas together?

To take parts and pieces that don't belong together and arrange a forced marriage of sorts.

If we've done our jobs right, we've covered the conference room walls and screens with incredibly smart thinking.

Big, fresh ideas that are hard to walk away from.

Like a kid in a candy store. Everything looks tasty.

This is a great place to be. We owe our clients our brightest thinking. Big and broad. Work that challenges them to make tough choices.

We also owe them our understanding of how ideas work.

Great ideas are singular and simple. They come from a common place.

Just as dachshunds and dalmatians weren't meant to breed, ideas need to remain pure.

[DISCIPLINE]

No genetic rewiring please.

But choosing one campaign direction doesn't mean discarding the rest of your thinking. It's all smart and on strategy.

Find ways to put those ideas to use. Maybe a blog or social post. Maybe it's a stunt. Maybe it's an idea that can be tucked away for another time and another use.

When we mash ideas together, they lose their identity. They become the stitched sum of their parts and pieces—not a singular idea.

Monsters belong in the movies. Let's leave it that way.

PRECEDENTS

New clients are like new dance partners. Figuring out the steps isn't always easy.

We don't want to step on toes or trample over feet, but we need to find a rhythm.

We also need to set some guardrails.

Wooing and winning new clients is the exciting and energizing part. With the ink still drying on the contract, the last thing you want to do is rock the boat.

But too often, bending over backwards early on puts you in a tough position.

It establishes expectations of how the relationship is going to work. It sets the ground rules.

Remember this: You have the opportunity to set some rules as well.

For any creative (or agency for that matter), establishing how you respond to client suggestions—especially on creative matters—is critical.

You'll often hear clients say, "You're the experts."

Okay, then you should act like it. Don't be afraid to stand up

[DISCIPLINE]

for what you believe in. Push back respectfully. Challenge your client.

Not every copy suggestion should be taken as a mandate.

Not every question requires being answered on the spot.

Give yourself time to think, explore and come up with the right solution.

If needed, remind your clients that's why they hired you.

You can be respectful and honest. As well as, stubborn.

You can't push back on everything. Then you just look like a spoiled creative brat. Client suggestions, at times, can actually make the work better.

Be open-minded and smart about where and when you draw the line. If it's something that doesn't really affect the creative, then it's not a hill worth dying on.

Save your powder for more important battles.

Precedents set expectations from both sides of the client-agency aisle.

Get the dance steps in place early because they're likely not going to change.

FINDING WHAT'S RIGHT

No idea is invincible. They can all be poked, prodded and picked apart like leftover holiday turkey.

Finding fault is the easy part and for some, that seems like their full-time job.

Here's something to consider: Start with looking for what's right about an idea. That's where the strength lies.

Searching for where the magic lies is what the sharpest minds on both sides of the agency-client table do.

What makes the idea unique, different and memorable?

What makes it demand that people drop what they're doing and pay attention?

Great ideas don't walk in quietly. They barge in, tracking mud, setting off alarms and creating a stir.

That kind of entrance can make some people nervous. But it's that edge, that part that makes you refuse to look away that is the essential ingredient.

It's just the right amount of spice to give the idea some bite.

Finding what's right requires guts. It means pushing past the "what ifs" and "someone could have a problem with that."

[DISCIPLINE]

Our job isn't to create wallpaper for the masses. We're not hired to generate background music.

We're here to sling lightning bolts that leave a permanent impression.

If we're going to succeed, we're going to have to ruffle some feathers and raise a few eyebrows.

That starts with finding what's right about an idea.

PITCH PERFECT

An agency owner once told me: "If you're asked to pitch a government account and don't already know it's yours, don't bother. Someone else has already been promised the rose."

Cynical? Sure.

Accurate? More often than not.

New business pitches are a bit like Vegas. Bright lights. Glitzy. Alluring. But the odds are often stacked against you. Be smart. You don't have to play every hand.

Be disciplined about where you place your time, energy and creative efforts.

Remember, pitches aren't mandatory. They are often a cattle call of agencies meant to impress board members.

The best agencies play by their own rules.

They don't answer every RFP. They self-select.

Organic growth from existing clients is always the best route. Referrals also provide a personal connection that can lead to trust and opportunity.

Sooner or later, however, you will need to beat the proverbial bushes.

[DISCIPLINE]

Although I often proclaim, "Category experience shouldn't count for everything." In truth, in pitch situations, it does count for something. A little reassurance in the client's mind that you're not starting from scratch.

Experience is usually a foot in the door. Your creative work can kick that door wide open.

New business prospecting is hard. You can't and shouldn't chase everything. It burns resources and creates frustration.

Pick and choose your opportunities carefully. Stack some wins, even small ones. They feed agency morale.

Don't be afraid to turn down pitches that don't feel right.

Every "no" clears the path for a better "yes."

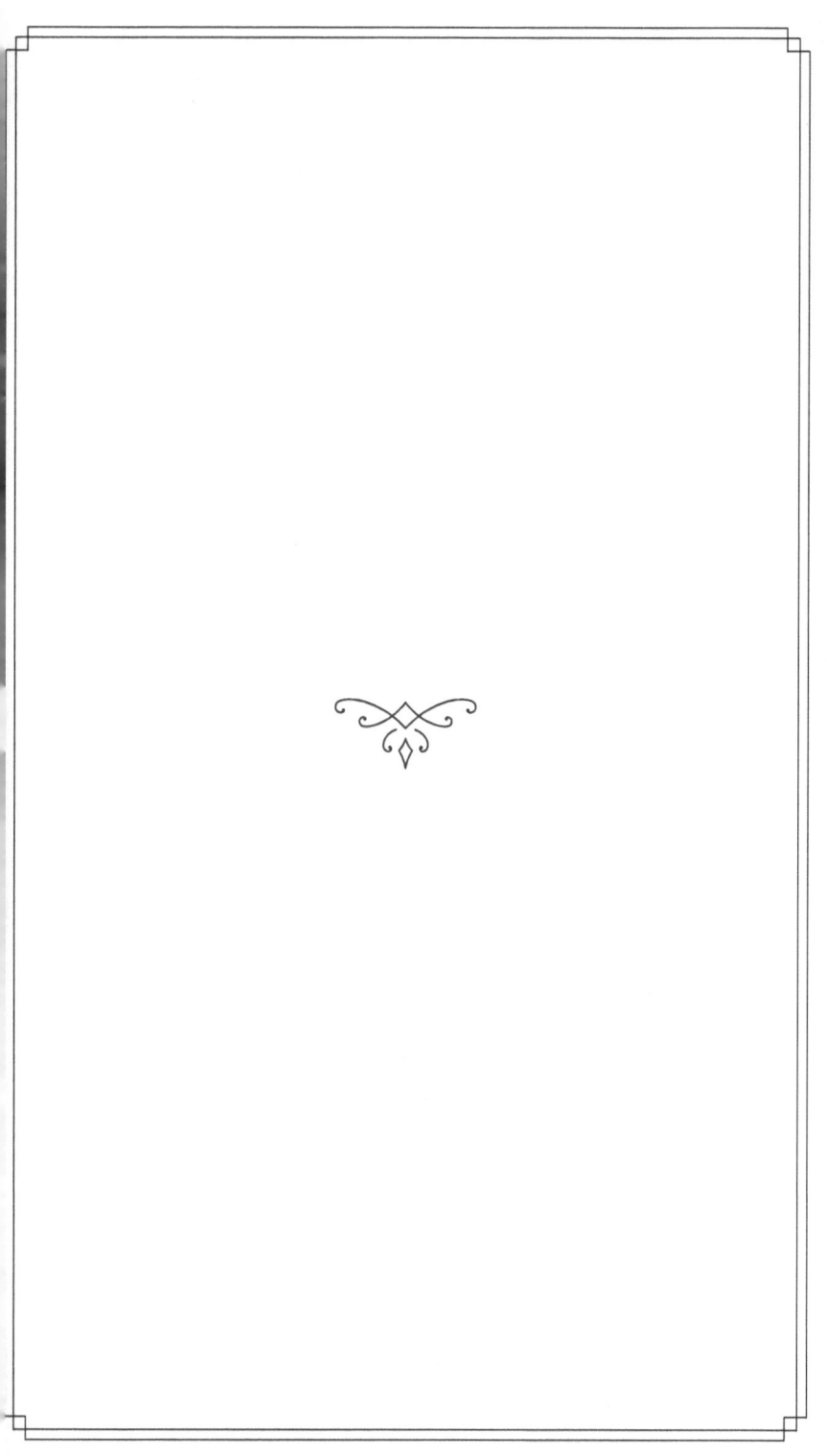

Step 10

INGENUITY

You can prepare, rehearse, but even the best laid plans will go awry. Be ready to think on your feet.

MAKING LEMONADE

Concepting is controllable. You decide what, where and when to share ideas. But once you move into production—especially on TV or video concepts—a lot is out of your control.

When things shift, be prepared to play the hand you're dealt. No whining, no excuses, just think fast. Work in this business long enough and you'll know this to be true.

To demonstrate the neck-snapping acceleration of the Mercedes-Benz 400E, we had a fun concept where we created the illusion that the car was being fired from a cannon.

The storyboards captured a sleek, black Mercedes, literally blasting along a pristine stretch of road. Sun setting in the distance, plush green foliage hurtling by.

The shoot was scheduled for Napa Valley, California. A golden countryside adorned with ripe vineyards and a kaleidoscope of summer colors.

They say it never rains in Southern California, but apparently the same can't be said for Northern California.

We arrived for the shoot only to find a dense, soupy fog which had settled into the valley and wasn't budging for at least a week.

[INGENUITY]

We couldn't wait it out.

Instead of beautiful sunsets and golden light dancing off grapevines, we were handed a bucket of lemons.

Then it hit us: "What if we shoot it in black and white?" Instead of the pristine approach we imagined, what if it was stark and edgy, but still captivating and elegant.

The client agreed and we found renewed energy and enthusiasm for our 'Plan B.' We loaded the camera onto the rails affixed in the 'barrel' of our prop and fired away.

As luck would have it, the thick trees lining the road were painted white from ground up to about six feet and as they whizzed by they resembled guardrails along a drag strip.

The result was stunning.

It wasn't part of the original plan, but the execution was flawless and made a dramatic statement.

We wrapped the shoot with a toast of lemonade, well-spiked.

THINKING INSIDE THE BOX

Everyone screams for 'out of the box' thinking. It sounds rebellious. Inventive. Downright death-defying.

But creativity actually thrives with structure and focus.

Ernie Schenck, legendary writer and creator of the *Strange Alchemy* newsletter, explains in his book, *The Houdini Solution*, how confines and constraints actually help us think faster, better.

If you haven't read it, you should.

To deliver great ideas, creatives need parameters. Bullseyes to aim at with out of bounds lines clearly marked.

Direction like, "Don't worry about production budgets. We're just looking for great ideas," doesn't help.

An idea that can't be produced within the budget is just a pipe dream in a pitch deck.

The worst thing we can do is bring our clients ideas they can't afford to do right.

So let's start there.

Can we afford a photographer or are we dealing with stock shots? Do we have the budget for a three-day video shoot or

[INGENUITY]

likely only a day? It all matters.

Which brings us to the creative brief. That's the box where it all starts. A smart, concise brief isn't a straightjacket, but a launching pad.

It shouldn't just check boxes, it should outline exactly who we're trying to reach, their mindset and exactly what we want their takeaway from our message to be.

I was careful there not to say, "Exactly what we want to tell them."

No one likes being told what to think, people want to arrive at their own conclusions.

Beyond production budgets and what makes our target tick, our 'box' should include clear objectives, realistic timing, and a well-honed tone of voice, among other things.

Knowing where the boundaries are actually makes creative concepting easier.

Ideas that don't fit in the box can easily be dismissed.

While ideas that are working are more easily spotted.

SKYWRITING

Clients love their brands. They love to see them, touch them and talk about them. Sometimes incessantly.

The sooner we accept that, the smarter off we'll all be.

From a creative standpoint, putting the product front and center can feel a little pedestrian. Too easy. It's the low-hanging fruit.

We've all seen blatant product placements enough to make us bleary-eyed, non-believers.

Worse yet, is seeing a super-sized brand logo open a commercial. Like we're all sitting on the edge of our couch eagerly awaiting the next message from Febreze or Enterprise Rent-A-Car.

Smart advertising doesn't work that way.

Still, finding a way to make the product the hero is essential. How does it benefit the consumer? What's in it for them?

When you find a way to convey that in a compelling, entertaining way, creative skies open up.

Beechcraft builds airplanes of all shapes and sizes. We were hired to develop a campaign promoting their Beechcraft Starship, which featured a unique wing design and engine

[INGENUITY]

placement that delivered an incredibly smooth ride.

If you've ever been bounced around a small cabin like a pinball, you'll agree that a smoother flight and less kidney damage is a compelling argument.

To prove our claim, we hired a calligrapher and sent her into the wild blue yonder. Her mission: handwrite our ad copy at 10,000 feet in mid-flight.

The headline read: *"Exactly how smooth is the ride in a Starship? This ad was written in one."*

The body copy began: *My pen is a Montblanc Meisterstuck. My paper, a Starwhite Vicksburg Tiara. And my seatbelt is securely fastened. Yet, perhaps more pertinent, my writing surface is perfectly still.*

The handwritten copy was a work of art in itself. Long-form, surrounding and framing the Starship in mid-flight.

The client saw their prized aircraft center stage, put on a pedestal. We saw a simple concept that not only made our client salivate, it made award show judges swoon.

If you don't think great work can build brands and also win awards, your head's in the clouds.

ANIMAL KINGDOM

Not all clients are created equal. And that's fine. They each play a role. Some keep the lights on and the paychecks clearing. Others give you the chance to make jaw-dropping, award-winning work.

A lucky few do both.

Picture your agency's client roster as a pyramid. At the bottom, the foundation: your big clients. They crank out a steady flow of projects. Not always glamorous, but reliable, and that assuredness keeps the rent paid.

These are your blue whales—massive, slow-moving, but capable of delivering needed cashflow and visibility.

Move up a tier and you'll find the stalkers. Let's call them leopards. They're not scrappy startups—they've proven themselves in the wild— and they're agile enough to pounce. These brands hunt market share, devour smaller competitors and have the hunger to climb.

These leopards are the sweet spot. They're challenger brands. Restless. Fearless. Obsessed with visibility. They're stalking the #1 spot, and they know bold creative can get them there.

For an agency, this is where the work gets fun.

[INGENUITY]

Finally, perched at the very top of the pyramid: the peacocks. Flashy. Dazzling. Head-turners. They may not bring in buckets of revenue, but they give your agency something priceless—work that stops people in their tracks and builds your reputation. Work you'll still brag about years later.

The trick to survival? Balance. A healthy mix of whales, leopards and peacocks. The whales fund stability. The leopards fund growth. The peacocks fund your reputation for outstanding creative work.

In the agency jungle, variety isn't just the spice of life—it's the difference between thriving and extinction.

A STATEMENT WIN

Great brands have agencies lining up at their door like beggars to a banquet. And why not? Every great brand knows you want a bite of their business.

But getting their attention isn't easy.

For months, we'd been trying to get into PING Golf. But how does a scrappy East Coast shop get the attention of a CMO sitting 2,000 miles away in Phoenix?

Cold calls? Straight to voicemail. Dropping by unannounced? Yeah, right. We needed a stroke of genius.

It came when I found a gently used set of PING irons in a pro shop. The price was right, so I swiped my Amex and tossed them in my trunk.

Then the light bulb went off.

What if Dan Harris—the guy ignoring our calls at PING—saw that I'd put my money where my mouth was?

I copied my Amex statement, circled the PING purchase in big red Sharpie and scrawled a note: *"Love my new PING irons. I would love even more to work on your brand."*

I folded up my statement and slid it securely into an envelope bound for Phoenix.

[INGENUITY]

And then… crickets. Days passed. Back to business as usual. Honestly, I forgot about it.

Until one afternoon, my phone rang.

"How do you like your new irons?" the caller posed.

No introduction. No nothing.

Irons? Who the hell was this?

Again: "Your PING irons—how do you like them?"

Now the dots began to connect for me.

"I love them," I smiled to myself.

He continued, "This is Dan Harris at PING Golf. I got your note. I'm impressed with your agency's work. We'd love to meet you in our Phoenix headquarters."

Jackpot.

I practically sprinted down the hallway to tell the team: we'd cracked the vault. Within weeks, PING was officially on our client roster. A monster win.

Sometimes in this business it just takes one swing.

Tee it high and let it fly.

SACRIFICIAL LAMBS

Clients need to kill things. Ideas, that is. That's okay, it's part of the process.

Sometimes getting the idea you really want across the finish line is less a straight shot, more a game of cat and mouse.

Creative concepting always yields a wide range of ideas—some bold, some safe, some just plain weird. Clients expect to see the spread.

But be careful what you bring to the table.

There's an unwritten rule in creative presentations: Never present an idea you wouldn't be happy to produce.

Because that's the one they'll pick.

If you're smart, you'll feed the lions a few sacrificial lambs. Some easy kills.

Toss in an idea that's a little too spicy, a little too edgy. One you'd actually love if it survived, but you know it probably won't. Clients usually swat those away with a, *"Wow, that's really out there, maybe too much for us."*

Perfect. That kill helps steer the conversation toward the work you actually want them to choose.

[INGENUITY]

My creative director, Kerry Feuerman, used to say: *"You have to trick clients."* Not in a shady, used-car-salesman way—more like Hansel and Gretel.

You lay down a breadcrumb trail that leads them to your strongest idea.

The beauty of showing a wide range is that it proves you've done the work. You've flipped over stones. You've explored. They've gotten their money's worth.

When you walk in with only one or two ideas, clients immediately think: *That's it? What else you got?*

The hard part, often, is deciding which ideas to share. Some clients will grab the safest option and never let go—so don't even show it. Bring them bold, relevant, surprising work. Just not boring.

Know your client. Know their appetite. And always stack the deck with work that can truly impact their business. Ideas you'd be thrilled to see out in the world.

And if a few lambs have to die along the way? So be it.

NETWORKING

This is not a business for cave dwellers. Yet the mere mention of networking is enough to make most creatives' skin crawl.

Either we're too introverted, too busy, or just too damn cool to stoop to that type of glad-handing nonsense.

But I will tell you that networking is a noble and needed pursuit.

Over the years, I've met future hires, potential clients, production partners of all kinds and slew of other ad types by showing up at industry events.

Talented people I most likely would have never crossed paths with otherwise.

Sure, I've thought more than once about bailing on these gatherings. Maybe stay on the couch, watch baseball and devour a sleeve of Oreos.

But every time I've gotten off my keister and ventured out, I've returned home glad I did.

Networking isn't just about building out your LinkedIn connections. You're also growing your personal brand. People don't really know you until they meet you. If you're lucky, they walk away thinking, *I'd like to work with that person someday.*

[INGENUITY]

I'm not advocating that you clear your calendar for every Coffee and Concepts, Marketing Mixer, or Happy Hour bash. That would drive any of us to drink.

Pick and choose when, where, and who. Say "yes" to a select few, then honor your word and show up.

Sure, it comes with a price. You'll have to endure endless small talk, business-card pushers and a buffet of chicken skewers growing tougher by the minute.

Basically, all the reasons we hate these kinds of events.

But somewhere down the road, those handshakes and conversations will pay off.

The relationships you build in this business will speak for you long after you leave the room.

Make sure they have good things to say.

Step 11

GRATITUDE

Life as a creative can be brutal,
but it beats a shovel and a hard hat.
Celebrate often, be grateful
and keep creating.

A POCKETFUL OF HOPE

The early morning sun came seeping through the windows of our handsomely-adorned beach cottage.

Welcome to paradise.

Our Creative Director, Rick Ender, had somehow convinced the agency brass that we needed to escape from the agency confines to focus on the NAPA Auto Parts TV assignment.

Our escape led us to a nice three-bedroom rental home on the sugar-sand beaches of Destin, Florida, about four hours south of Atlanta.

Yes, a boondoggle in its greatest sense.

Rick and his partner were working on the big, national TV campaign. Concepts that would lead to an expensive shoot in LA, working with an A-list director and sleeping in the 800-thread-count sheets of a swank Santa Monica hotel.

My creative partner, John Boone, and I were tossed the table scraps – a smaller assignment with likely little to no production budget.

No LA. No five-star hotel on the beach. No per diems.

Knowing our budget constraints, John and I devised an incredibly simple concept using animated type treatments.

[GRATITUDE]

But for our little concept to see the light of day, we still had to run a gauntlet of hole punchers and second-guessers.

We worried that storyboards alone might not capture the magic of our little brainchild.

That's when Rick, our boss, reached into his pocket, pulled out his checkbook and a Hail Mary.

"Let's just produce the sucker," Rick suggested.

Wait? Before we even show it to the client?

We called a production partner who loved the ideas so much, they offered to produce all three executions for $500.

Rick's pen couldn't hit paper fast enough.

By presenting the finished spots, not just storyboarded ideas, there was no leap of faith necessary.

No "Imagine if you will."

Funny. Smart. Simple. Sold.

The campaign was included in the *Communication Arts Advertising Annual* and an early springboard for my career.

Thanks, Rick.

BOOMERANGS

The best gifts in this crazy advertising life are the ones you never see coming.

We spend our days head down, noses to the grindstone, churning, sweating to meet deadlines.

There's rarely time to look up, let alone look back.

Years fly by as you're ping-ponging between new agencies, new cities and new responsibilities.

It's a marathon made up of countless sprints where catching your breath feels like a luxury.

People often talk of 'giving back' once the craziness ends. The dust on their career settles, time frees up and deadlines are no longer breathing down their neck.

But giving back actually happens every step of the way.

A short time ago, I ran across a short film posted on LinkedIn. Sharp. Funny. Beautifully crafted.

It was written by a copywriter at Wieden+Kennedy. I clicked on his profile and was surprised to find that, like me, he was a Grady grad from the University of Georgia—a fellow bulldog.

So I sent him a note. Told him he didn't know me, but I'd

[GRATITUDE]

love for him to come back to Athens and speak to a class of students.

His reply started with a curveball:

"Hi Ron, actually I do know you. You were a guest speaker in one of my UGA classes years ago. I've followed your work ever since. I'm a big fan."

What? I had a fan club? Even if it's just one, I'll take it.

We spend our careers launching ideas out into the world. We make ads, sit on panels and podcasts, lead workshops and more.

We rarely know what sticks and what doesn't.

But every so often, our words, actions and goodwill come circling back to us.

WARDROBE. CHECK.

From the outside, a life in advertising can look downright glamorous. Wining and dining clients. Awards galas. First-class flights and five-star hotels.

But those of us on the inside know it's also sleepless nights, unreasonable deadlines and clients who don't always see things our way.

But once in a while, this heartless industry tosses you a bone.

In prepping for a Lexus shoot, my creative partner and I were sent to Vail, Colorado, for a wardrobe check ahead of the shoot.

Wardrobe check? Really?

The concept featured a half dozen speed skaters, all dressed head to toe in black skin suits. Simple enough.

Did we really need to arrive a week early just to nod and say, "Yep, those look great."

Then it dawned on us.

Maybe all-nighters, soul-sucking meetings and files brimming with dead ideas deserve reparations.

Surely, we had some coming.

[GRATITUDE]

There was one small problem: two boys from south of the Mason-Dixon line were about to face the frozen tundra of the Western Rockies woefully unprepared.

Enter our broadcast producer, part guardian angel, part logistics ninja. Concerned for our survival, she found room in the budget to make sure we were properly outfitted and wouldn't suffer a cruel death from frostbite or exposure.

Soon, boxes started landing on our doorstep. Patagonia parkas, Sorel boots, Gordini GTX storm gloves, Smartwool Nordic Crew socks and KUHL Merino beanies.

Suddenly, the all-nighters didn't seem all that bad.

Doing the math, we had flights on Monday, wardrobe check on Tuesday and the shoot, not until the following week.

That's time to kill.

That's when our producer informed us that she'd arranged skis and lift tickets for Thursday and Friday.

This business will take you to a lot of places. Some, better than others.

When fortune smiles, don't hesitate to strap on a pair of Rossignol Rallybirds and send a little powder flying.

WAKE-UP CALLS

The sun was still creeping into the morning sky as I knocked on a heavy wooden door inside a gated San Antonio community.

No answer.

I knocked again.

I could detect the shuffling of feet, then the door slowly cracked open.

There I was, standing eye to eye with music legend George Strait—The King of Country himself.

George was wearing a blue terrycloth bathrobe and had traded his cowboy boots for wool slippers. He excused his appearance as he welcomed me in.

At the time, George was the spokesperson for Wrangler Jeans, and as creative director on the account, I was there to film him delivering a few inspiring words to the Wrangler sales team.

I sat in George's living room pinching myself, surrounded by Western sculptures by renowned artist, Frederic Remington. George's home was relatively modest, but perfectly adorned. Much like George himself.

[GRATITUDE]

I heard the approaching sound of boot heels on hardwoods and George soon reappeared in his signature crisp, white shirt and perfectly-starched Wrangler jeans.

A true pro, ready to take the stage.

George was the consummate gentleman and could not have been more accommodating.

The shoot went off without a hitch. Before I knew it, I was back on a plane bound for Richmond.

The advertising business will open a lot of doors for you. Sometimes, a country music legend is standing on the other side.

EXPLETIVES AND EXPLOSIONS

It started with a small bump, then harder. *Bam!* From my rearview mirror, I could see the driver behind me laughing maniacally.

What the hell, it was just a rental car.

The ramming continued. *Bam!* I kept my foot pressed firmly on the brake as my white knuckles clung to the steering wheel.

Being forcibly pushed into the intersection, through a red light, wasn't my idea of fun.

Bam! Bam! Bam!

Was this some guy's idea of a sick joke?

Actually, yes.

Long before director Michael Bay was blowing up things on the big screen with *Pearl Harbor*, *The Rock,* and *Transformers*, he was directing commercials.

His name was quickly on the rise around the L.A. production scene and we were lucky to squeeze onto his dance card.

We were warned, however, that along with his immense talent, came an ego to match. As we would find, it was

[GRATITUDE]

Michael's world and we were all just living in it.

Our shoot was for the Lexus SC400 and was tailormade for Michael. A pornographic parade of sheet metal rushing by at 100 miles per hour. Like everything Michael touched, it required you to strap in and hold on tight.

The concept was simple: The SC400 would race down an open road leaving a trail of leaves spinning in its dust. The twist was the car cleared and the logo came up only 20 seconds into a 30-second spot, leaving the viewer hanging for the final ten seconds. The voiceover then suggested that with so much power under the hood, we might consider running shorter commercials.

Michael delivered a great shoot and amazing footage, making his practical jokes and oversized ego more than tolerable.

We'd survived the intersection encounter with only minimal damage to our rental car's bumper. My guess is it wasn't the first time the production company had to cover for Michael's antics.

Sometimes, shooting with the best requires risking life, limb and bumper.

BE A SPRINGBOARD

Most of us spend the early years of our careers just trying to prove we belong. That we're smart, funny, clever. We're big league material.

But as you move up the creative food chain, it's no longer just about bringing out the best in yourself.

As titles and responsibilities grow, being able to motivate, direct, and shape the creatives on your team is critical.

It's not easy and not everyone has that gear.

At Team One, our creative boss, Tom Cordner, had assembled a wealth of creative talent. The lineup was stacked like the 1929 Yankees, a virtual 'Murderers' Row' of writers, art directors and designers.

Tom used to say, "I know I can't keep you forever." He said it with a grin, but he meant it.

When your agency's work starts lighting up the award shows, phones start ringing. Headhunters start circling. Resignation letters start quietly being drafted.

That's actually a sign of success.

When your people are in high demand, you're doing something right.

[GRATITUDE]

Great agencies build creative cultures where people can flourish. They make work that gets noticed. And, inevitably, so do the people who made it.

I've always loved that part of the job. Seeing creatives grow and succeed. Sure, loyalty is great, but it shouldn't be a prison sentence.

To continue evolving, creatives need new environments, new challenges.

Tom's "can't keep you forever" line was a very pragmatic and realistic view. It stripped away the emotion and ego that can make departures feel like betrayals.

All you can do is to build a creative culture so special that people don't want to leave. And if they eventually do, hopefully they walk out the door better than when they came in.

That's not a loss.

That's legacy.

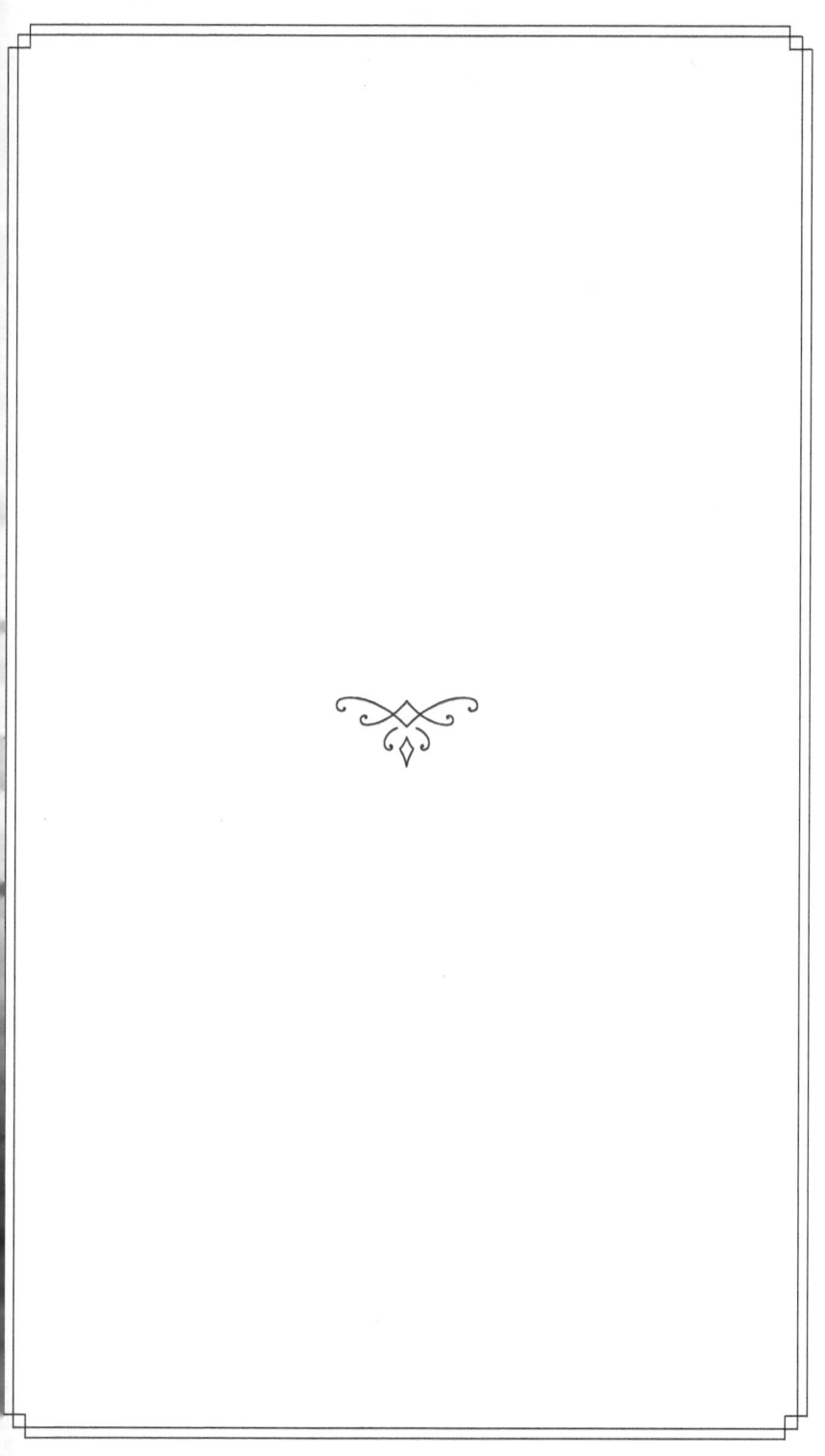

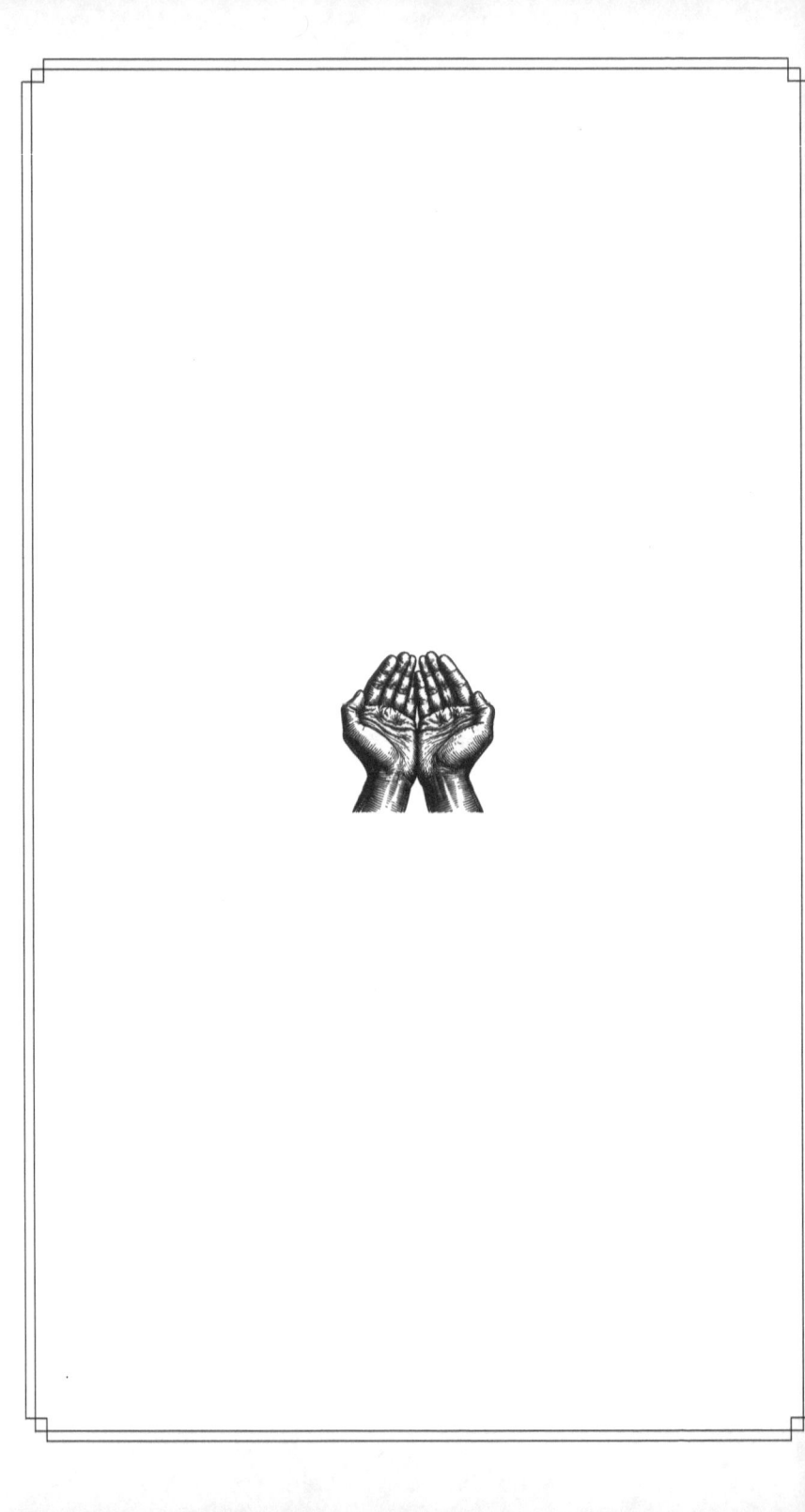

Step 12

ACCEPTANCE

Your life as a creative is unscripted.

People and places will all shape your story.

It's okay to be okay with that.

LOVE OVER MONEY

As the clock struck midnight, I sat on a well-worn living room couch in Chestnut Hill, Pennsylvania.

Jerry Cronin, an advertising idol of mine, sat next to me as we shoveled praline ice cream and whiskey into our mouths, listening to Stevie Ray Vaughn wail on Little Wing.

Wieden+Kennedy had recently won the Subaru account and needed a writer with automotive experience.

Someone who could wrap their head around anti-lock braking, dual climate control and fuel-injection.

Someone possibly like me.

With a stomach full of butterflies, I flew from L.A. to Philly to interview for my dream job working with Jerry, Vince Engel and the small team at W+K's upstart East Coast office.

While I loved Jerry and Vince, I didn't love Philadelphia. But I knew that before my flight from LAX lifted off.

Still, this was an opportunity of a lifetime to have Jerry as a mentor, add some Subaru work to my portfolio and maybe a ticket back to W+K HQ in Portland, Oregon.

I could put up with a few years of cheesesteaks and Eagles fans for that.

[ACCEPTANCE]

But this decision wasn't a slam dunk. Along with the aforementioned distaste for most things Philly, I was also in a relationship.

Yes, there was a girl.

A girl I liked very much and who was, most likely, not signing up for Philly.

Who could blame her?

The return flight from Philadelphia to Los Angeles felt a bit like a time warp, but within seconds after our tires left the runway, I knew I would not be returning to the City of Brotherly Love.

I was turning down the job I had chased for years for a greater opportunity.

Six months later I was engaged. Now, over 30 years later, I'm still happily married.

Life is full of choices. All of them are right.

THE KILLING FIELDS

The grasslands of the Serengeti are littered with the bleached-white bones of the fallen.

The tired, the weak, and the lame for whom survival was not meant.

Over 1.5 million wildebeest thunder across the plains each year in the Great Migration, moving in a massive loop across Tanzania and Kenya.

It's a breathtaking spectacle, but also a brutal one. Many won't make it.

Feels a lot like advertising, doesn't it?

We spend our days and nights delivering ideas, herding them into decks and marching them straight into battle. Like those wildebeests, many will perish.

Some are picked off early. The obvious, easy targets. Others are ambushed farther along the trail by budget cuts, politics and more.

It's a war of attrition and that's the point: Only the strongest, fiercest survive.

Your ideas will face a gauntlet and it starts between your ears. You're the first executioner. The judge and jury.

[ACCEPTANCE]

Be hard on yourself, because everyone else will. That includes your creative director, your account team and your client.

No shortcuts here.

Weaning off your weakest ideas will reveal the strengths of your strongest ones. It will help shape your rationale for the ones you recommend. Killing off ideas clears and unclutters your creative landscape.

Clarity and commitment around your ideas builds confidence and conviction.

Approaching each assignment looking for a needle in a haystack is a fool's errand. Instead, put as many wildebeests on the trail as you can.

Because, as we know, there will be many predators along the way.

Protect the strongest ones. The ideas capable of leading to big places. In the end, that's what everyone wants.

MULLIGANS

Few things feel better than seeing your idea make it through the meat grinder of approvals and into the real world.

But even when the work is out there, tiny things will gnaw at you and nibble at your brain.

A line you'd tweak. A cut you'd stretch. A color grade you'd nudge. Things you wish you could revisit. Little ghosts whispering, *It could have been better.*

In golf, it's called a mulligan—a do-over, so to speak.

For me, it's usually a word or a line of VO that never sat right in my ear. You could tweak it forever. Truth is, few things are nailed on the first try. Or even the fifth.

Here's the good news: your audience will never notice. Those tiny 'imperfections' that keep you up at night? They fly right past everyone else. What's done is done.

Even when you 'sweat the details,' you'll miss a few. Everyone does.

As I write *Advertisers Anonymous*, I know there will be lines, even whole entries, I'd like another crack at. But there are no mulligans here.

When famed Beatles' bassist, Paul McCartney, penned "*And*

[ACCEPTANCE]

in the end, the love you take is equal to the love you make," he must've flashed a toothy grin knowing he'd nailed it.

Only a few years later, he gave us, "*Some people want to fill the world with silly love songs, what's wrong with that?*"

C'mon, Sir Paul. Need a mulligan?

That's the deal with creativity. You push. You polish. You obsess. And eventually, you have to print it, export it, ship it.

Chase perfection, sure. But recognize it rarely exists outside of unicorns and hindsight.

Execution certainly matters. Big concepts matter more.

In truth, those "flaws" you're losing your mind over? They're just pimples on an elephant's ass.

And you're the only one staring.

DEATH AT 30,000 FEET

Our flight home from Greensboro, North Carolina, was barely airborne when cocktails clinked in celebration.

We'd just finished a marathon push for Wrangler Jeans, capped by a presentation that felt like a home run. Weeks of late nights and early mornings had led to this.

Finally, we could exhale.

The meeting with Wrangler's VP of Marketing, Brian Goldberg, and his crew could not have gone better.

We presented five campaigns, each greeted with smiles, laughter and nods of approval.

The air in that stuffy conference room had turned into pure oxygen.

For a few shining hours, this was why we were in this business.

The tough call was theirs now: which campaign to choose. But that was a champagne problem. We already had the taste of production in our mouths.

By the time our Beechcraft King Air touched down in Richmond, the sun was sinking toward the horizon. We grabbed our bags, swapping director wish lists and potential shoot locations.

[ACCEPTANCE]

That's when our Account Executive, Ann Hendley's, phone rang.

"Hi, Brian. Yeah. Okay. Uh-huh."

Her side of the call was maddeningly vague. We waited for the smile, the fist pump, the news that we'd scored.

Instead: "It's all dead."

Silence.

Wait—what?

Every campaign. Every laugh. Every head nod. DOA. No explanation. No feedback. Just dead.

That's the cruel side of this business. Just when you think you've nailed it, the hammer swings back on you.

Ideas will die. Sometimes without reason or warning. But new ones will live, too. Often against all odds.

The hope is that, over a career, the balance sheet evens out.

But at 30,000 feet, sipping bourbon in plastic cups, we thought we were untouchable.

Turns out, gravity works on ideas, too.

MIND IN THE GUTTER

Some things you just can't see coming.

So unexpected, so improbable that you can only scratch your head, throw your hands up and laugh out loud.

We were working on the launch of the Lexus ES300. The baby brother to the LS400. Sleek. Stylish. Sophisticated. Born with the same DNA as its older sibling. Just in a smaller, more affordable package.

The creative brief couldn't have been more direct: show how the ES300 shares the same genes as its older brother.

Mission accepted.

Our initial print ad featured the ES300 poised on a bluff at sunset. A stunning image captured by photographer Michael Rausch. It felt majestic, like automobile royalty.

The headline read: *It was born with a silver dipstick in its mouth.*

Boom. Creative brief nailed.

Fast-forward a few weeks. Launch date looming. Ad materials were fast on their way to *Road & Track*, *Car & Driver*, *The Wall Street Journal*, *Business Week* and a long list of others.

[ACCEPTANCE]

"Dipstick" as we affectionately called it, was about to make its grand debut.

When the magazine issues hit our desks, we were eager to see our handiwork in its full glory.

There was only one small problem.

Our headline stretched across the gutter, or center section, of the magazine. Meaning we needed to allow room on the mechanical for letters that might disappear into the gutter.

Apparently, we'd not allowed enough room.

As luck would have it, the word dipstick sat right in the crosshairs of the gutter.

At a glance, the headline read: *It was born with a silver dick in its mouth.*

Of all the words in the English language, that one? Of all the letters to disappear, those four? The gutter claimed the four center letters of the word dipstick. The odds were astronomical.

Mistakes will happen. Many out of your control.

If you can't keep your mind out of the gutter, at least keep your headline out of it.

A LETTER FROM THE PRIEST

Even the best creative work is bound to rub some people the wrong way. It comes with the territory and the sooner we accept that, the better.

Earlier, I shared the story of our ad for Mizuno's golf division, featuring a dozen golfers waiting in a confessional line.

A funny, unexpected visual that almost never saw the light of day.

Even though we'd gained approval from Mizuno's marketing team, we still had one last hurdle: We needed the approval of Mizuno USA's President, Bob Puccini.

Bob was a conservative guy. Not much of an appetite for category-busting creative work. A large beauty shot of a Mizuno iron with call-outs noting its technology breakthroughs was more in Bob's wheelhouse.

Gaining Bob's blessing would not be easy.

In our setup, we explained how Marketing Director, Dick Lyons, had commented that the iron's design and forgiveness made it almost impossible to hit a bad shot.

In Dick's words, "You almost feel like you're cheating." Dick's observation was our inspiration.

[ACCEPTANCE]

Then we unveiled our ad concept to Bob.

Bob sat in silence. He smiled. He acknowledged it was very clever. Then, as he squirmed in his seat, he explained that he was concerned about mixing golf and religion.

Especially here in the Bible Belt.

He was worried that Mizuno would get letters saying, "How dare you."

In all honesty, I told Bob, "You may get letters. But for every person who finds fault with this ad, you will have dozens upon dozens of golf enthusiasts, your target market, who absolutely love it."

Bob thought for a moment, then took a deep breath and said, "Let's do it."

A week into the campaign launch the letter came, landing squarely on Bob's desk.

It was from a priest in Chicago. He was hoping to get a poster-sized version of the ad to frame for his parish office.

Apparently, the good priest was a golfer as well.

THE GIFT OF CREATIVE SANITY

Your career will be marked with the remnants of ideas that never made it past the conference room wall. Beautiful, brilliant, heart-pounding concepts—shot down like stray dogs in the street.

It's brutal. And it wears on you.

Sure, you'll score some wins. You'll get stuff produced. Maybe even hoist a shiny trophy or two. But even your "victories" will come with fingerprints all over them. And they won't all be yours.

That's why every creative needs a side gig.

Not a hustle to pocket a few extra bucks. I'm talking about something creatively pure. Something that doesn't need approvals, insights, legal clearances, or ten people telling you they "like where it's going."

Just you. Raw. Unfiltered.

It could be music, photography, pottery, poetry, painting, perhaps a newsletter. Something to flex your creative muscles without constraints.

Let the day job pay the bills. Let the side gig keep you sane.

The truth is creative people are creative on all fronts.

[ACCEPTANCE]

Why limit yourself to ad-like objects?

My side gig has always been music. I've written over 100 songs. None of them are going platinum. None will buy me a beach house. But they make me grin like an idiot when I play them.

And that's enough.

No keywords for SEO. Just my words—good, bad, or ugly—left untouched.

Find your outlet. It doesn't matter if you're brilliant at it. It doesn't matter if anyone ever sees or hears it. What matters is that it's yours. Uniquely yours.

Call it therapy. Call it rebellion. Call it whatever you want.

I call it a gift.

A GAME OF RECOVERY

Imagine a game that you can't master. Where there is no measure of excellence. No perfect game. Only falling short and failure.

I didn't know it at the time, but that's what attracted me to golf. It's an endless uphill climb. And, unlike Everest, there's no reaching the summit.

In golf, blame is easily spread. The wind blew your ball off course. There was a noise in your backswing. Your putt hit a pitch mark. You landed in a divot. Someone forgot to rake the bunker.

But most often, blame lies squarely in the mirror.

That's what I love about the game. It's just you, your tools, Mother Nature, and hopefully a bit of good fortune from the Golf Gods. It is a game where you must accept the consequences and go from there.

The inescapable truth is that few things go right in golf. That's why it's been called a game of recovery. Simply because you can't hit a great shot with every swing.

The same is true with advertising. Even your best creative shots can quickly find trouble with picky clients, unseen production obstacles and a host of other pitfalls.

[ACCEPTANCE]

So, what's next?

You can complain and point fingers. Or pull your collar tight around your neck, take dead aim and fire back. Hit the shot no one saw coming.

Some of my most rewarding moments on the course, as well as the boardrooms, have come when I quit feeling sorry for myself and got back to the business at hand.

Golf, and advertising, owe you nothing. If you want to be successful, you're going to have to take it.

ACKNOWLEDGEMENTS

I can't thank Ernie Schenck enough for his candid foreword. Not surprisingly, Ernie honestly and eloquently captured my exact intentions and hopes for this piece. Thanks to Kerry Feuerman, Diane Cook-Tench and Dan Balser for their generous endorsements. You guys make me sound better than I deserve.

You can't fly solo in this business and I'm very grateful to my closest art director partners, including John Boone, Joe Paprocki and Scot Crooker, for sitting countless hours with me staring at empty pages, hoping for magic to appear.

Thanks to all the immensely talented creatives and colleagues that I was fortunate to work with at The Martin Agency, Team One and other shops. I'm truly a product of those environments.

To our small, but mighty team at Huey/Paprocki where I spent some of the most fun and rewarding years of my career. Together, we accomplished amazing things, always punching above our weight.

To my partners at Buster, David Healy and Jon Voss. Thank you for your friendship, support and for rarely asking me to cancel a tee time.

Many thanks to the incredible team at Ripples Media. Specifically, Andrew Vogel and Nicole Wedekind for guiding me through uncharted waters. A huge thanks to designer Burtch Hunter for his dedication to the craft and for being a true creative partner throughout the design process.

Lastly, thanks to my parents, Ron Huey and Maxine Manning, my stepmother Rita Huey, my sister Paige Huey, my wife Judy Moran, and my children Alex and Nicholas Huey for your endless support.

ABOUT RON HUEY

How does a boy from Winder, Georgia make his way to Atlanta? Ironically, by way of Los Angeles and Richmond.

On the West Coast, Ron's creative work helped establish Lexus as the #1 automobile brand in the U.S. and put Ron's career in overdrive. His work soon caught the eye of The Martin Agency. In their hands, the keys to the Mercedes-Benz account. Ron's conclusion: time to trade in the Lexus.

After years in the trenches at some of the nation's top creative shops, Ron witnessed the birth of his own agency, Huey/Paprocki, and two weeks later (the birth of) his twins, Alex and Nicholas. How's that for pressure?

Creativity magazine named Huey/Paprocki one of their "Top 20 Agencies to Watch." Over the next seven years, the agency piled up over 300 awards, establishing itself as one of the Southeast's premier agencies.

Ron's creative campaigns have been recognized by *The One Show*, *Communication Arts*, *Cannes* as well as twice being named *MPA Stephen E. Kelly* finalist—recognizing the top 25 magazine campaigns of the year.

Ron has served on The Creative Circus National Advisory Board, Atlanta Ad Club Board, the University of Georgia's Grady College of Journalism and Mass Communication Board of Trust as well as authoring articles for *Communication Arts*, *Creativity*, *Adweek* and others.

Advertisers Anonymous is Ron's first book.

www.ingramcontent.com/pod-product-compliance
Lightning Source LLC
LaVergne TN
LVHW040041080526
838202LV00045B/3437